DIMITRI JELEZKY

FASHIONDESIGN

FIGURINES FOR FASHION DRAWINGS

PART 1

WOMEN FIGURINES

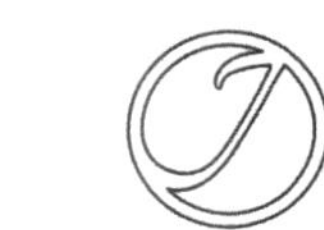

Jelezky Publishing, Hamburg 2014

Jelezky Publishing UG, Hamburg
www.jelezky-publishing.com

First English Edition, October 2014

The illustrations in this book were made by Dimitri Jelezky.

Layout, Cover ©dimitridesign.org

For further information on the contents of this book contact:

www.dimitridesign.org
info@dimitridesign.org

ISBN 978-3-945549-04-9

CONTENTS

PREFACE 6
PROPORTION RULES 7
CONSTRUCTION / REFERENCE LINES 9
FIGURINES 11
FACES 69
HANDS 75
FEET 79

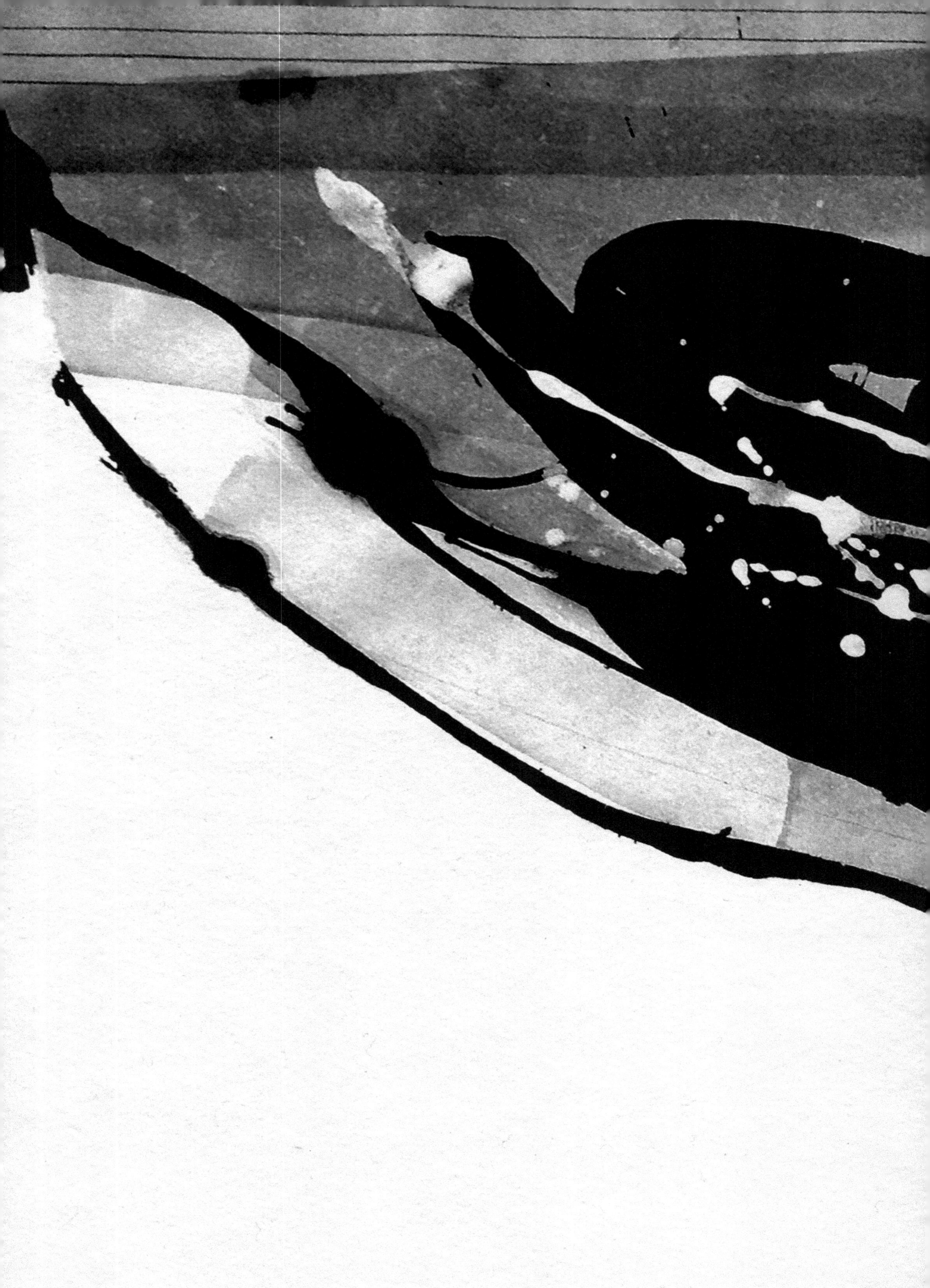

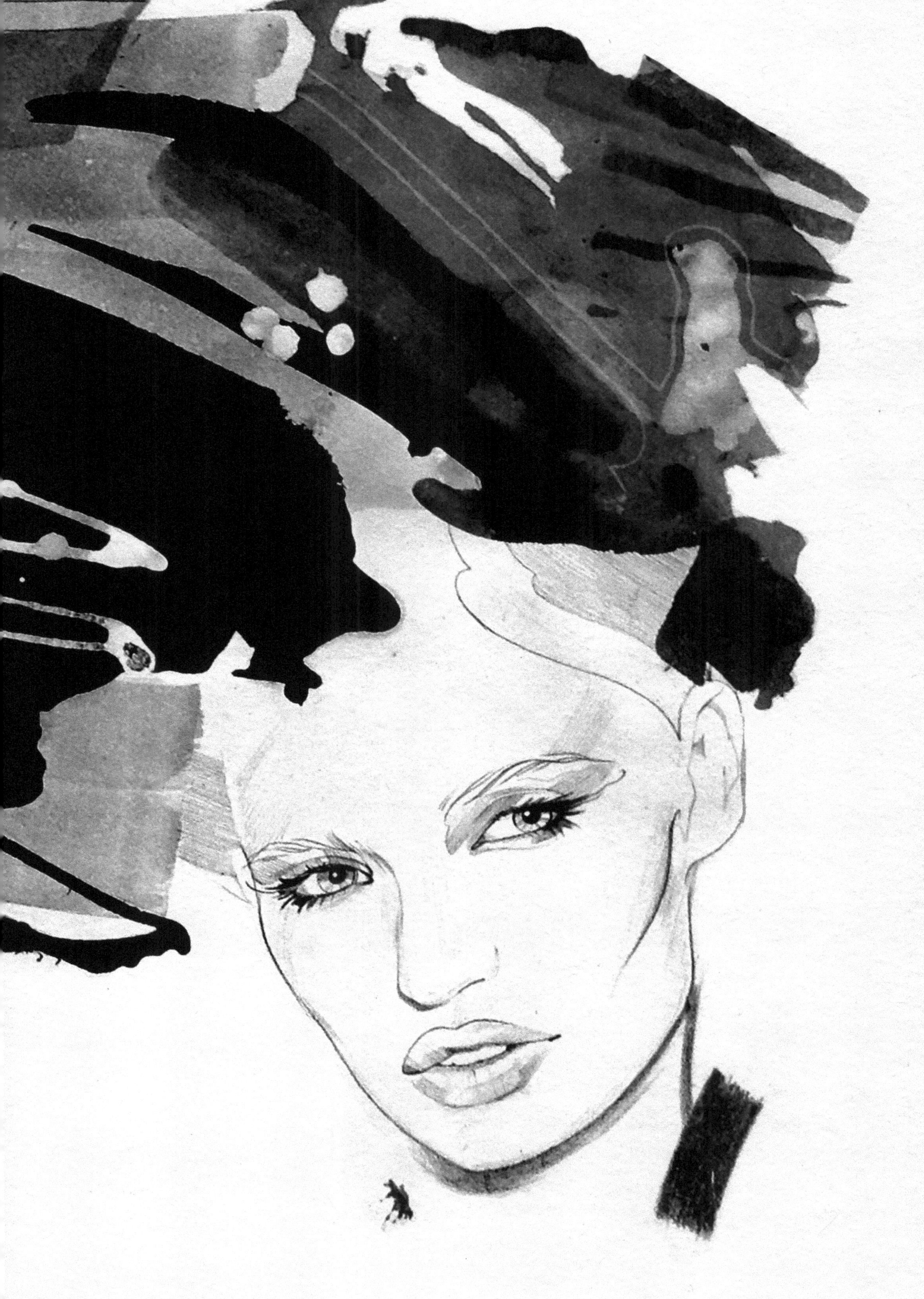

PREFACE

A fashion designer is primarily a „generator of ideas". The easiest way to make other people understand his ideas happens with the help of a fashion drawing on paper. The faster and better you are able to represent your ideas, the more effective and convincing your fashion designs appear. A beautiful, stylish fashion drawing always leaves a good impression on the viewer.

This book is an indispensable reference work for designers, illustrators, artists, students at design schools and people who are engaged in fashion design. The book includes templates for fashion drawings about 120 women figurines templates. In this book you will also find inspiring templates for hairstyle and representation of face, hands and feet. This book will help you to learn to create qualitative, casual and trendy fashion drawings independently.

PROPORTION RULES

8 ½ Proportions

In figurines for fashion drawings we use the classic specifications 8 ½ head length. The classic 8 ½ head figure proportion is wonderful for stylized fashion sketches. Of course you can use other stylistic directions for fashion drawings, for example 9 ½ head length, 10 ½ head length (especially for dresses), 11 ½ head length, etc. Please note here that „ ½ „ means that a figurine is wearing shoes with a high heel. If you, for example, draw shoes with a low heel e.g. ballerinas, then you use 8,9,10,11 head length figure proportions. All dimensions depend on the style of the fashion drawing.

The human body is mirrored, the right side is identical to the left side. The perspective and the volume of the body change our perception of the human form.

The equilibrium line or plumb line is important to build up the balance of the figurine.

The main pillar holds the whole figurine of visual perception. Therefore, I recommend to build your fashion drawings with simple design lines. That will help you to build up further figure poses by visualization quickly and effectively.

A walking figure creates an effect of dynamics. With that the impression of the "Catwalk" effect arises, as if the figurine runs the catwalk. That looks very trendy at the representation of your designs.

When you draw the clothes pay attention to the volume of the material, to pleats, to the fabric. Pleats can be stretched (depending on the material and figure posture). The pleats can also be very fluent, e.g. plisse pleats of dresses, etc. The rule is: observe and analyze.

It is a safe way to work with simple geometry. To divide the body into various cylindrical shapes can help you a lot when drawing the fashion figurine.

PROPORTION RULES

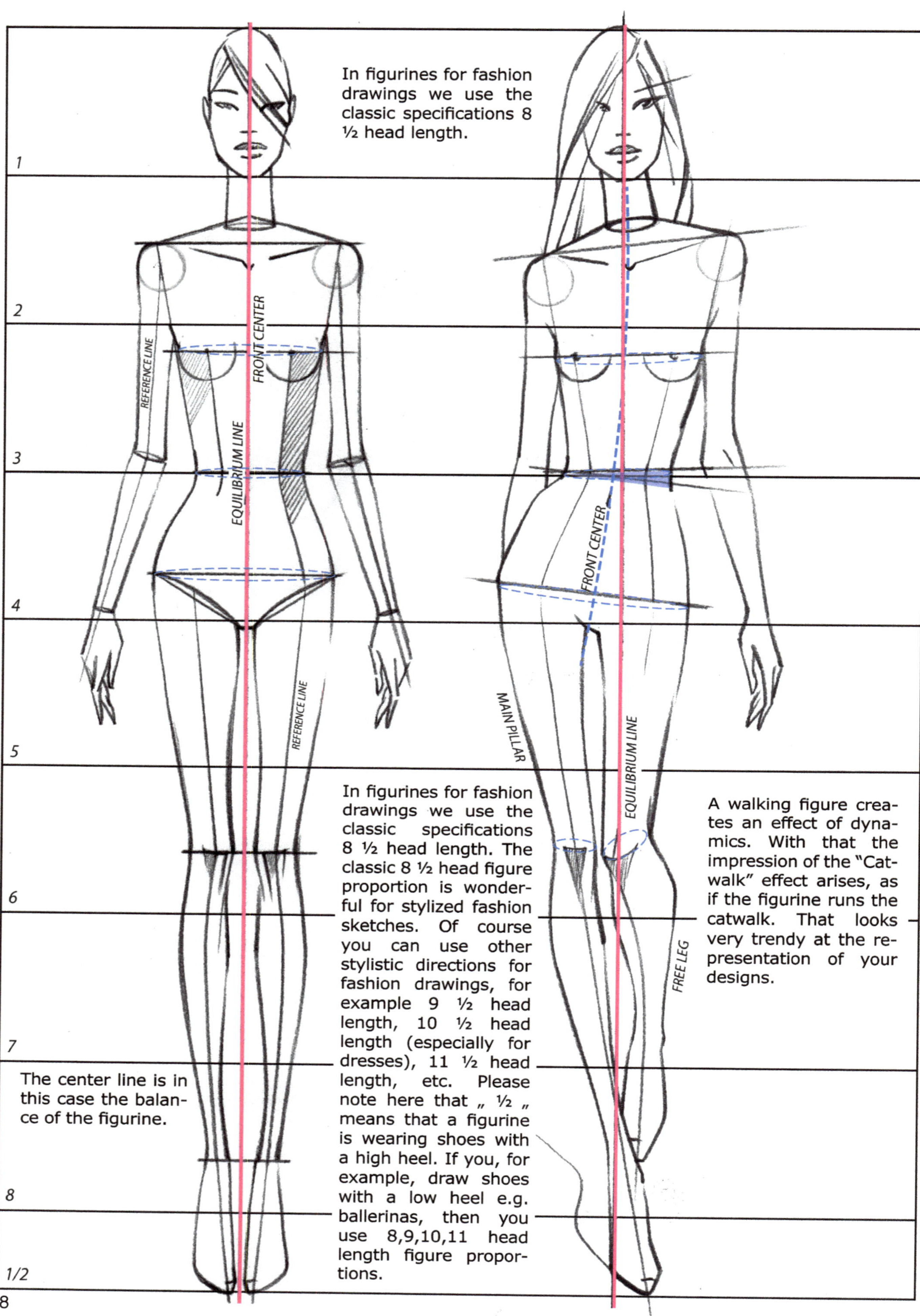

In figurines for fashion drawings we use the classic specifications 8 ½ head length.

In figurines for fashion drawings we use the classic specifications 8 ½ head length. The classic 8 ½ head figure proportion is wonderful for stylized fashion sketches. Of course you can use other stylistic directions for fashion drawings, for example 9 ½ head length, 10 ½ head length (especially for dresses), 11 ½ head length, etc. Please note here that „ ½ „ means that a figurine is wearing shoes with a high heel. If you, for example, draw shoes with a low heel e.g. ballerinas, then you use 8,9,10,11 head length figure proportions.

A walking figure creates an effect of dynamics. With that the impression of the "Catwalk" effect arises, as if the figurine runs the catwalk. That looks very trendy at the representation of your designs.

The center line is in this case the balance of the figurine.

CONSTRUCTION / REFERENCE LINES

When you draw the clothes pay attention to the volume of the material, to pleats, to the fabric. Pleats can be stretched (depending on the material and figure posture).

The pleats can also be very fluent, e.g. plisse pleats of dresses, etc. The rule is: observe and analyze.

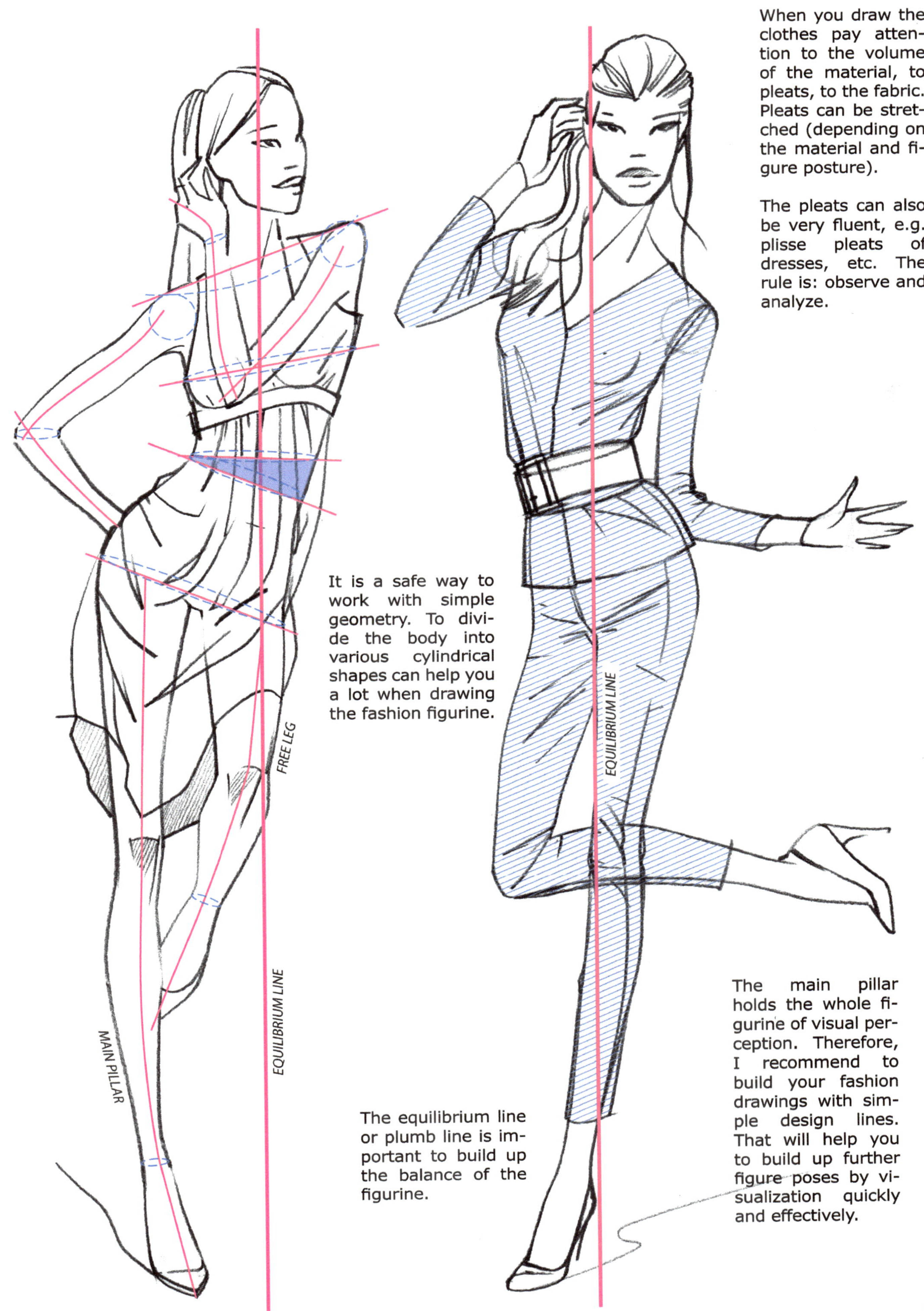

It is a safe way to work with simple geometry. To divide the body into various cylindrical shapes can help you a lot when drawing the fashion figurine.

The equilibrium line or plumb line is important to build up the balance of the figurine.

The main pillar holds the whole figurine of visual perception. Therefore, I recommend to build your fashion drawings with simple design lines. That will help you to build up further figure poses by visualization quickly and effectively.

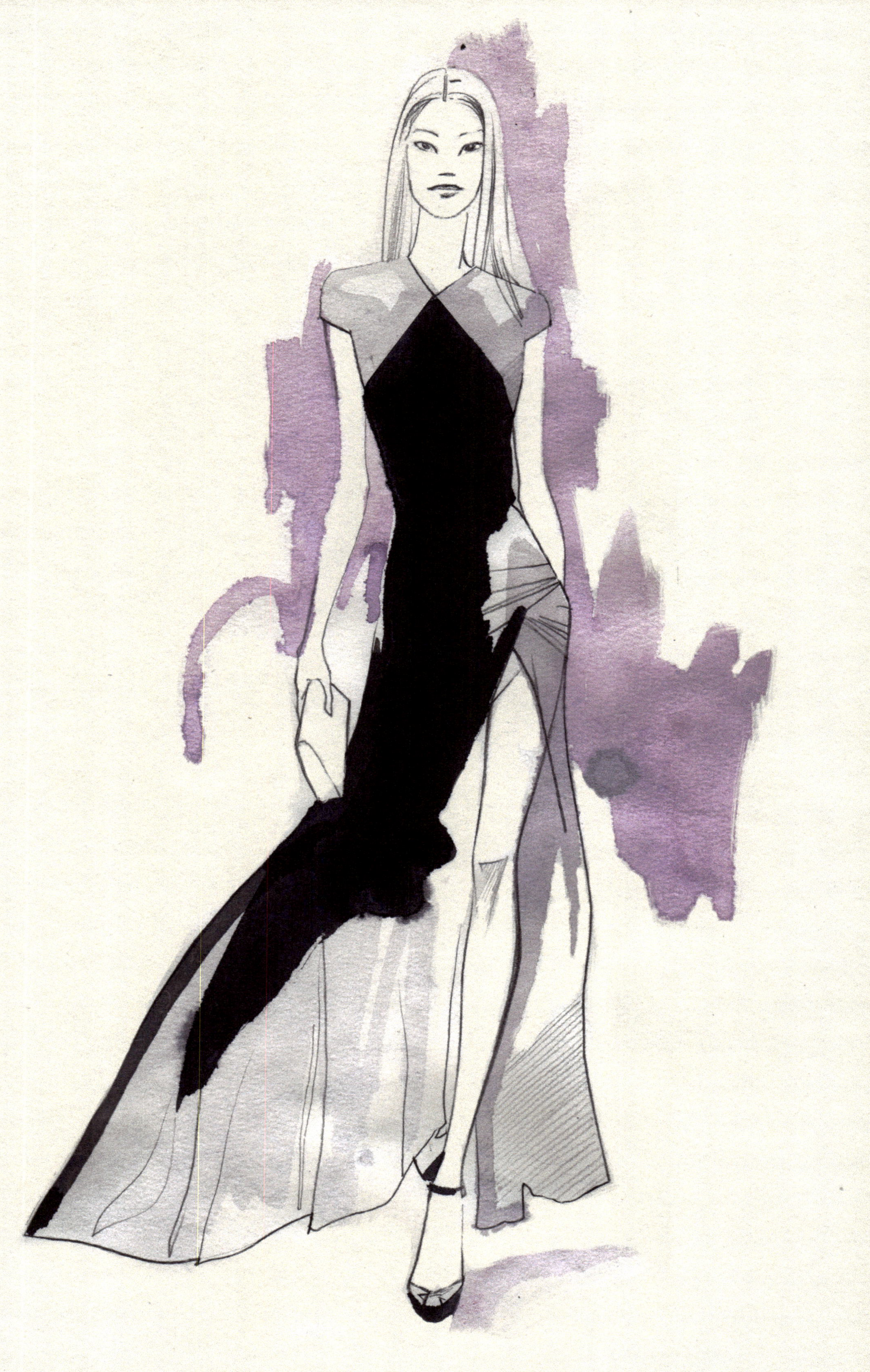

FIGURINES

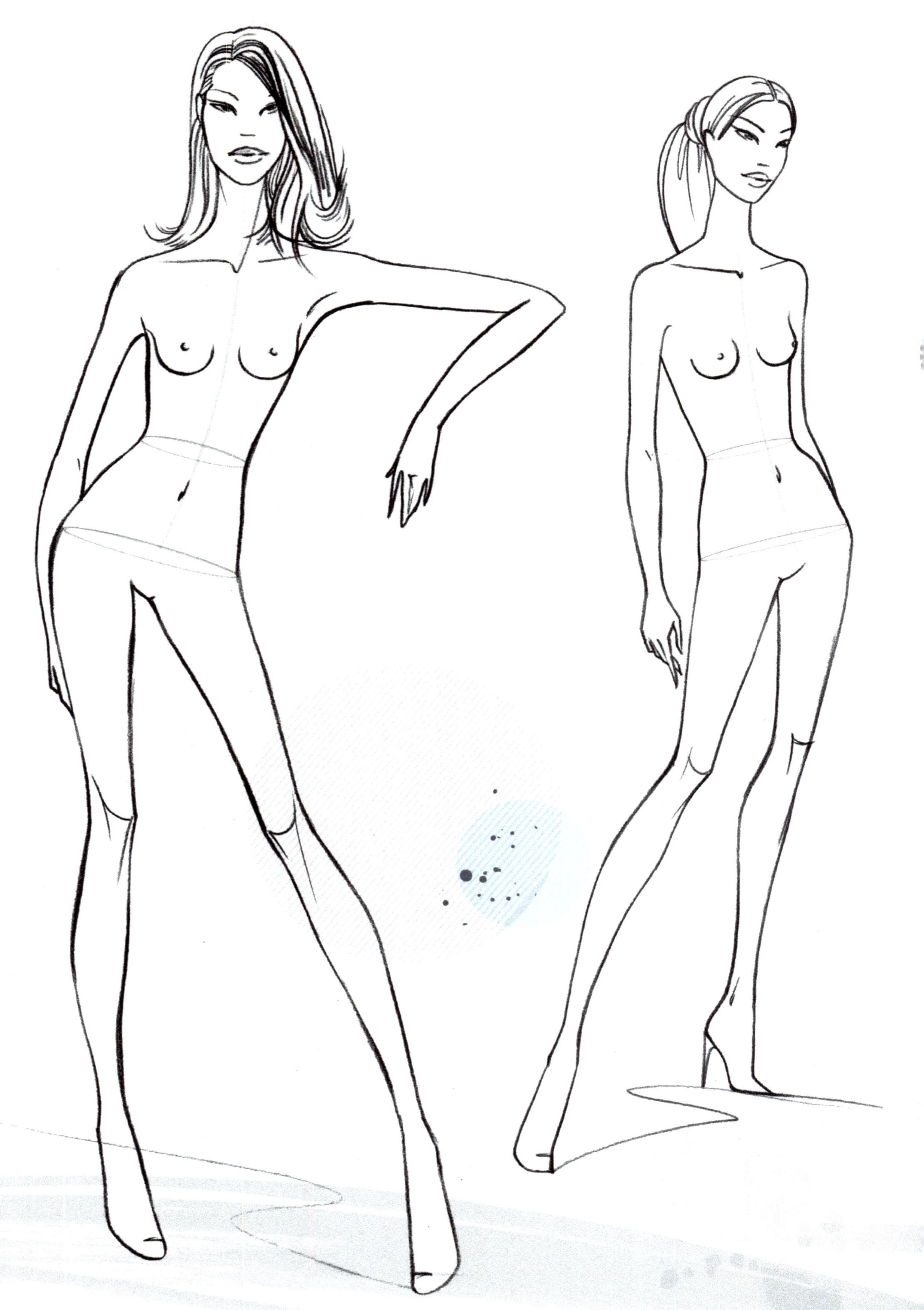

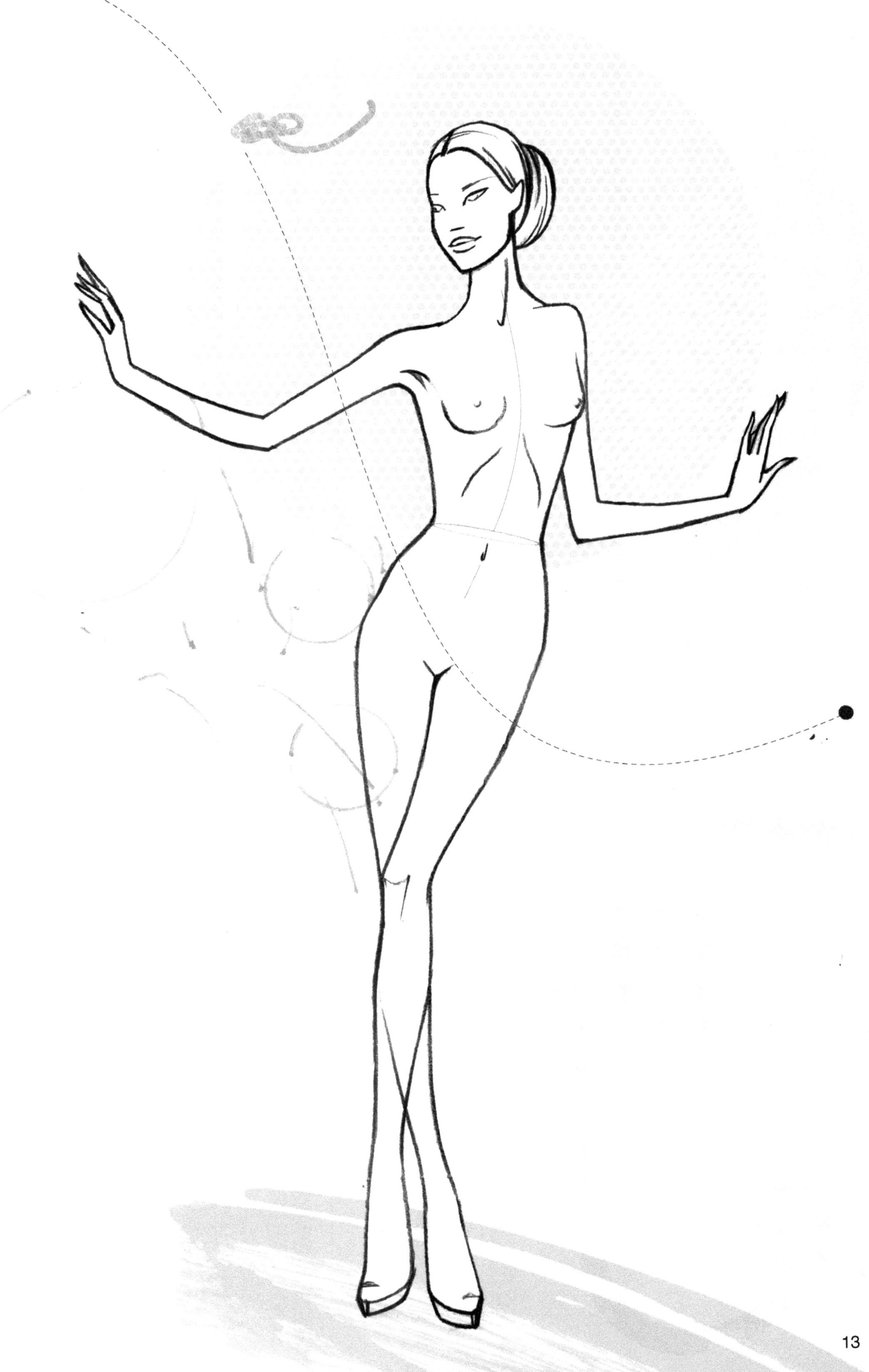

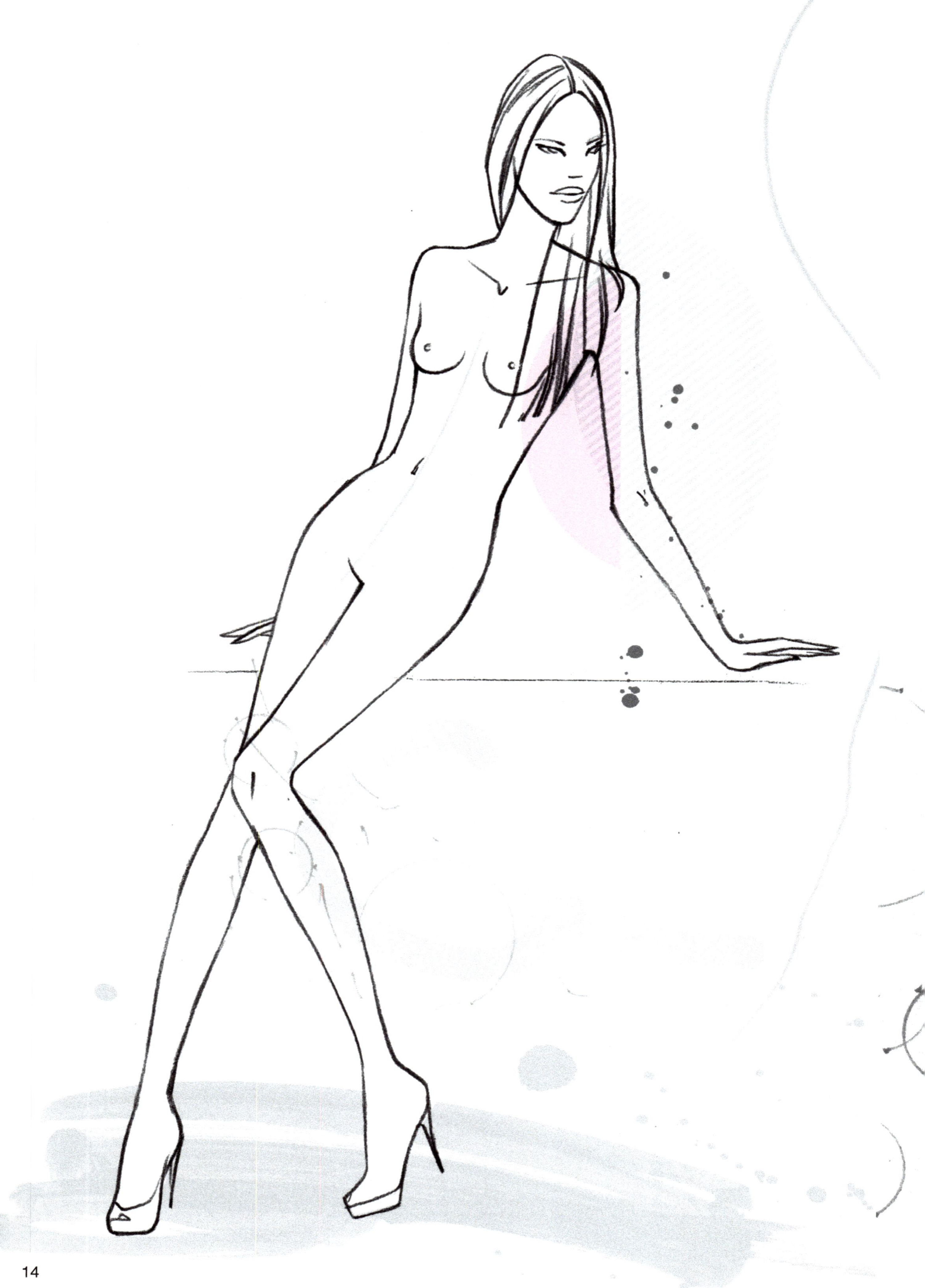

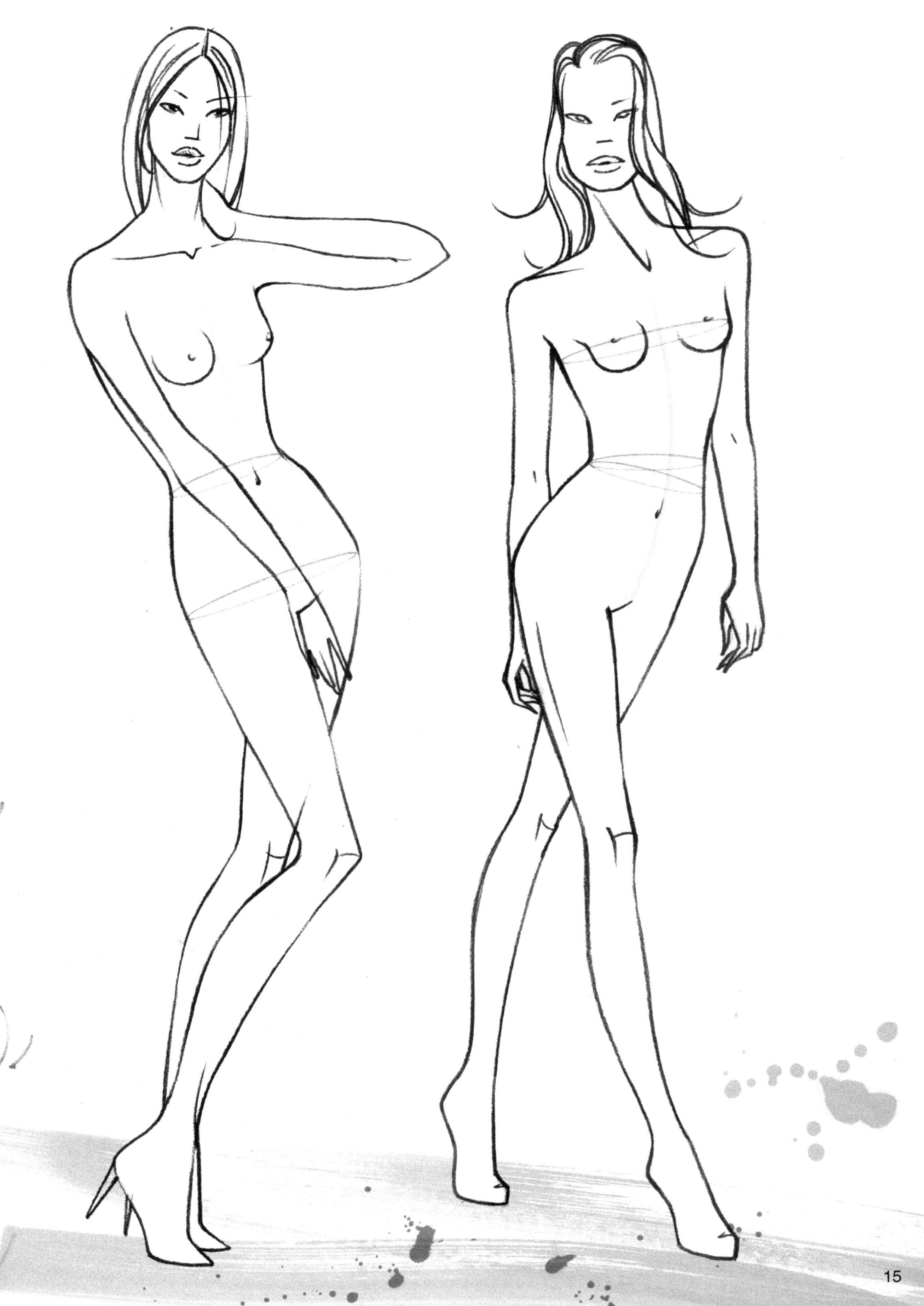

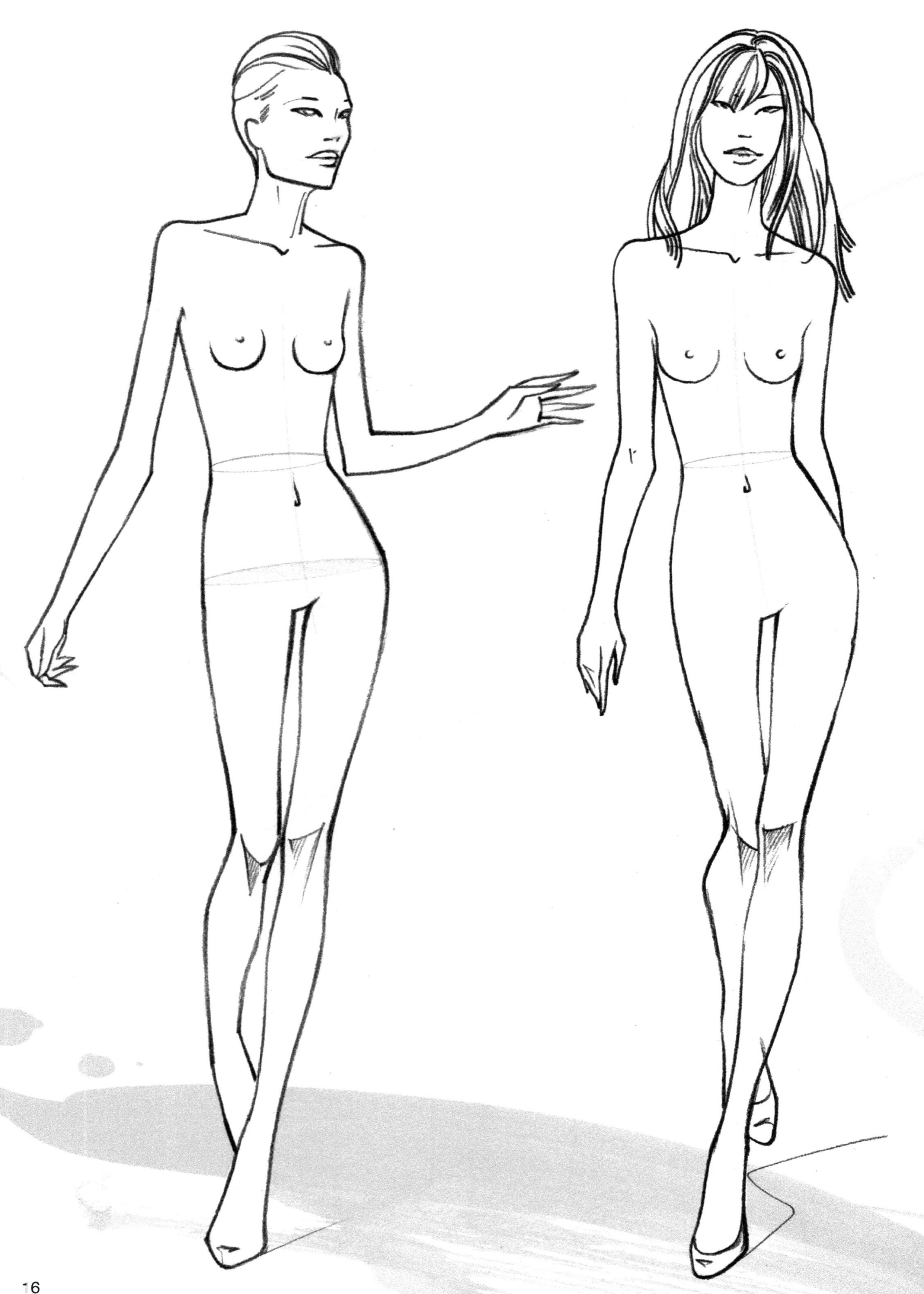

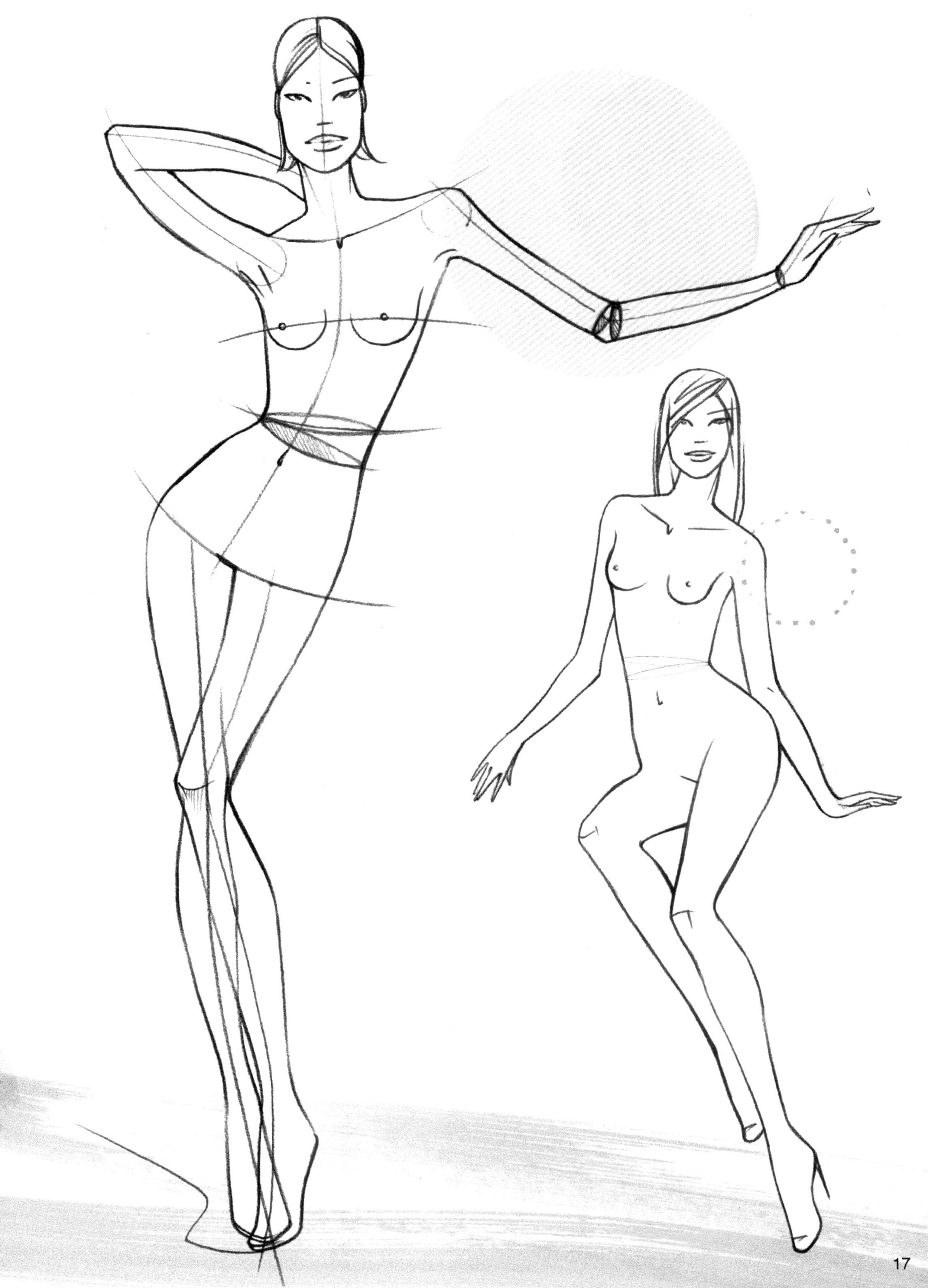

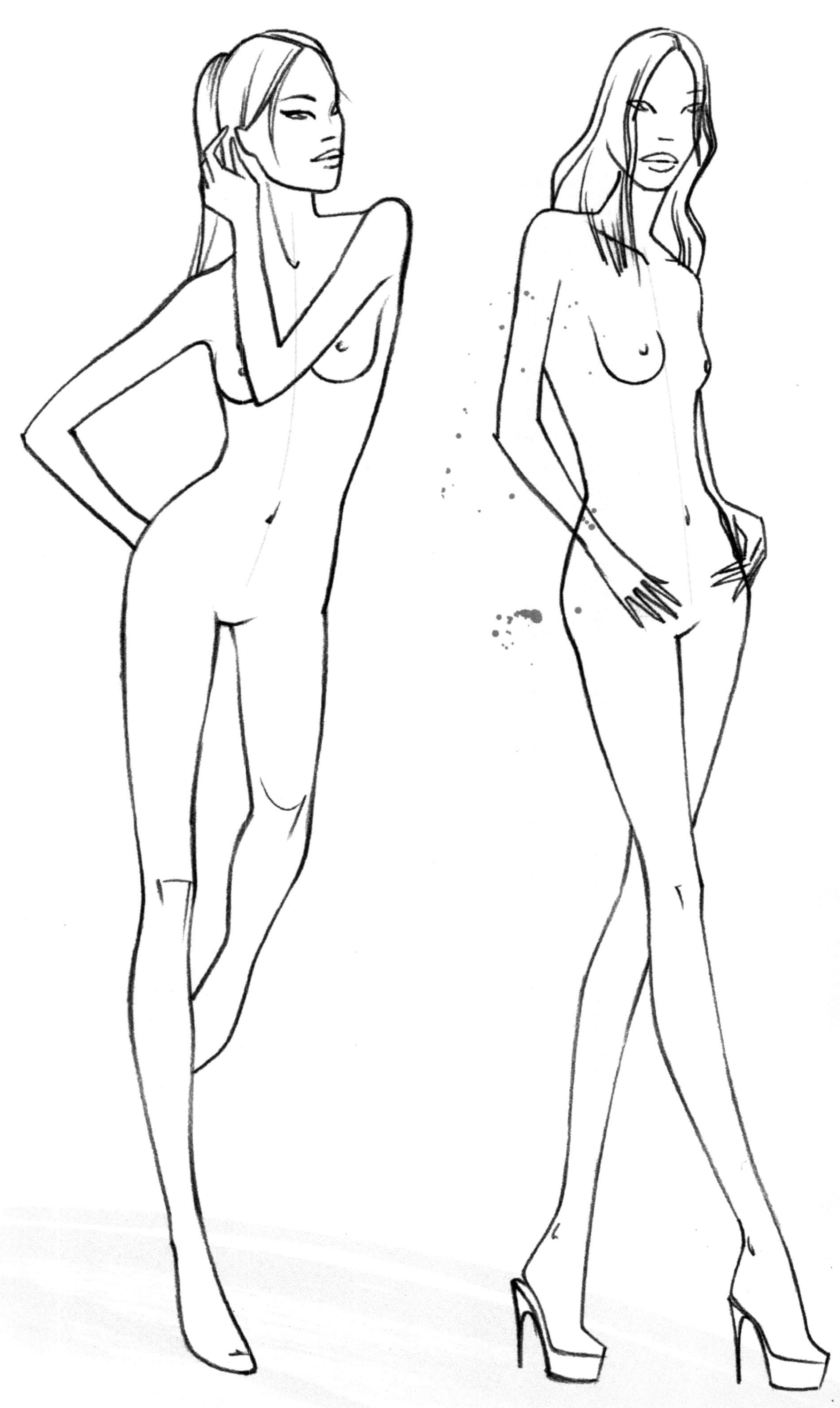

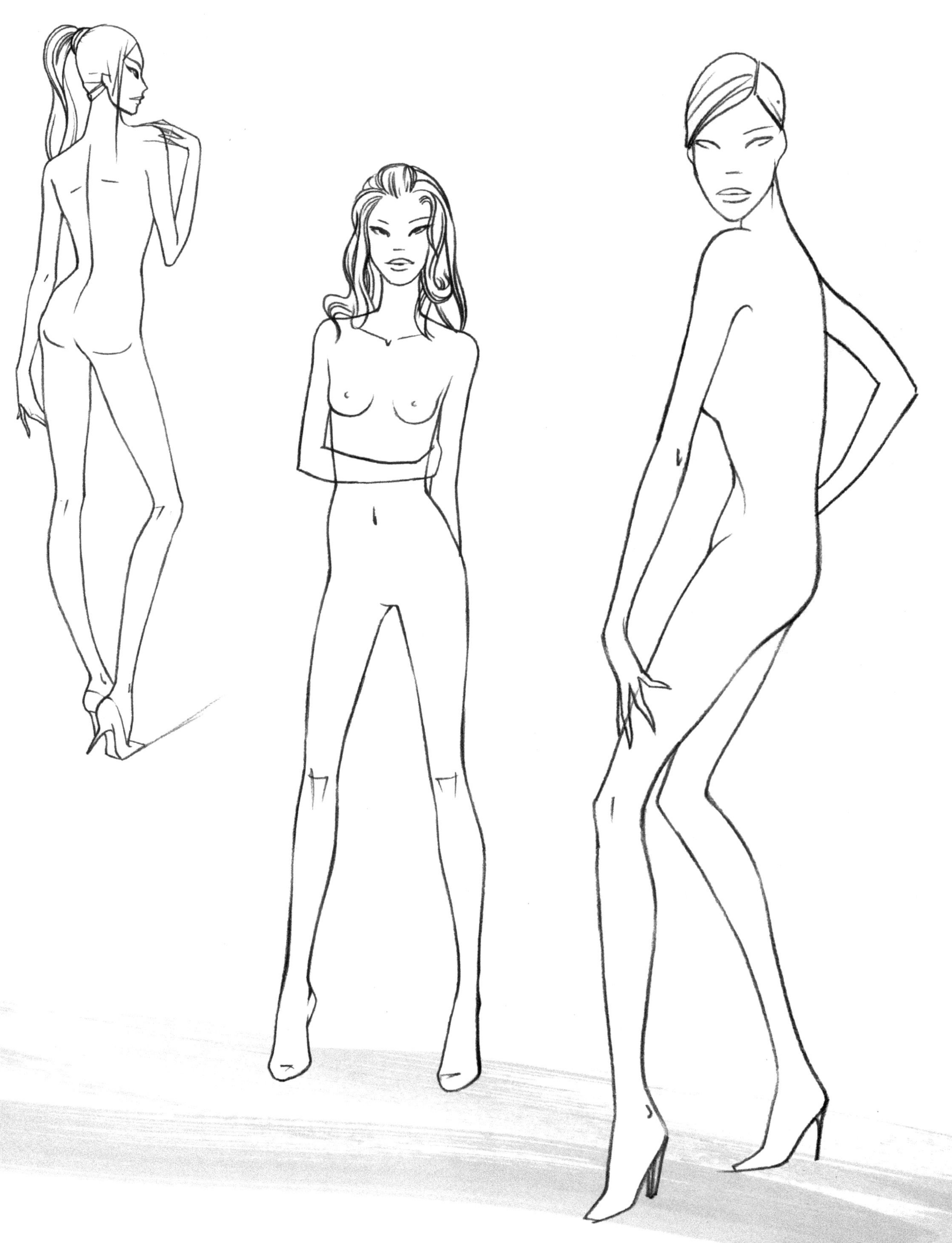

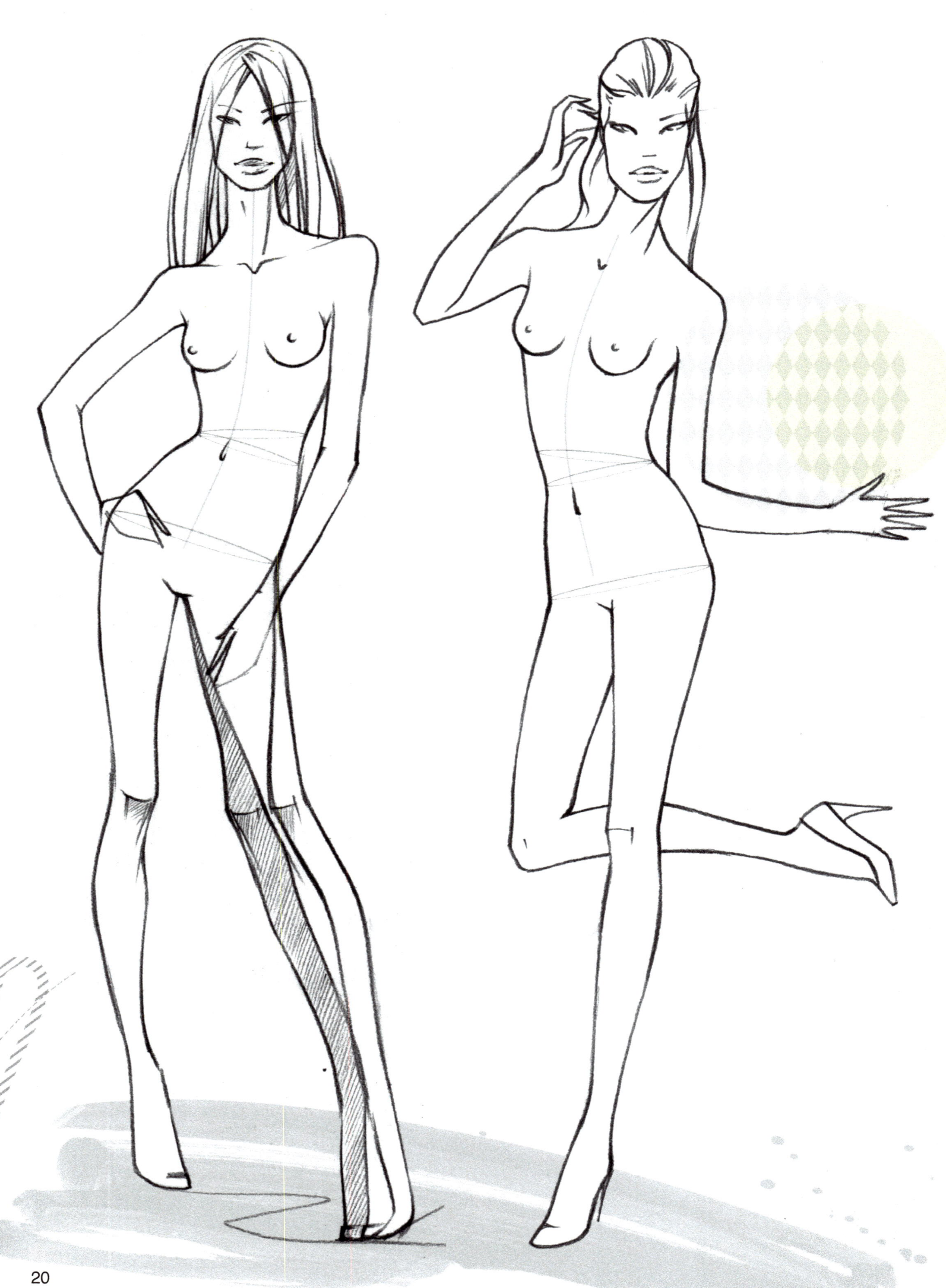

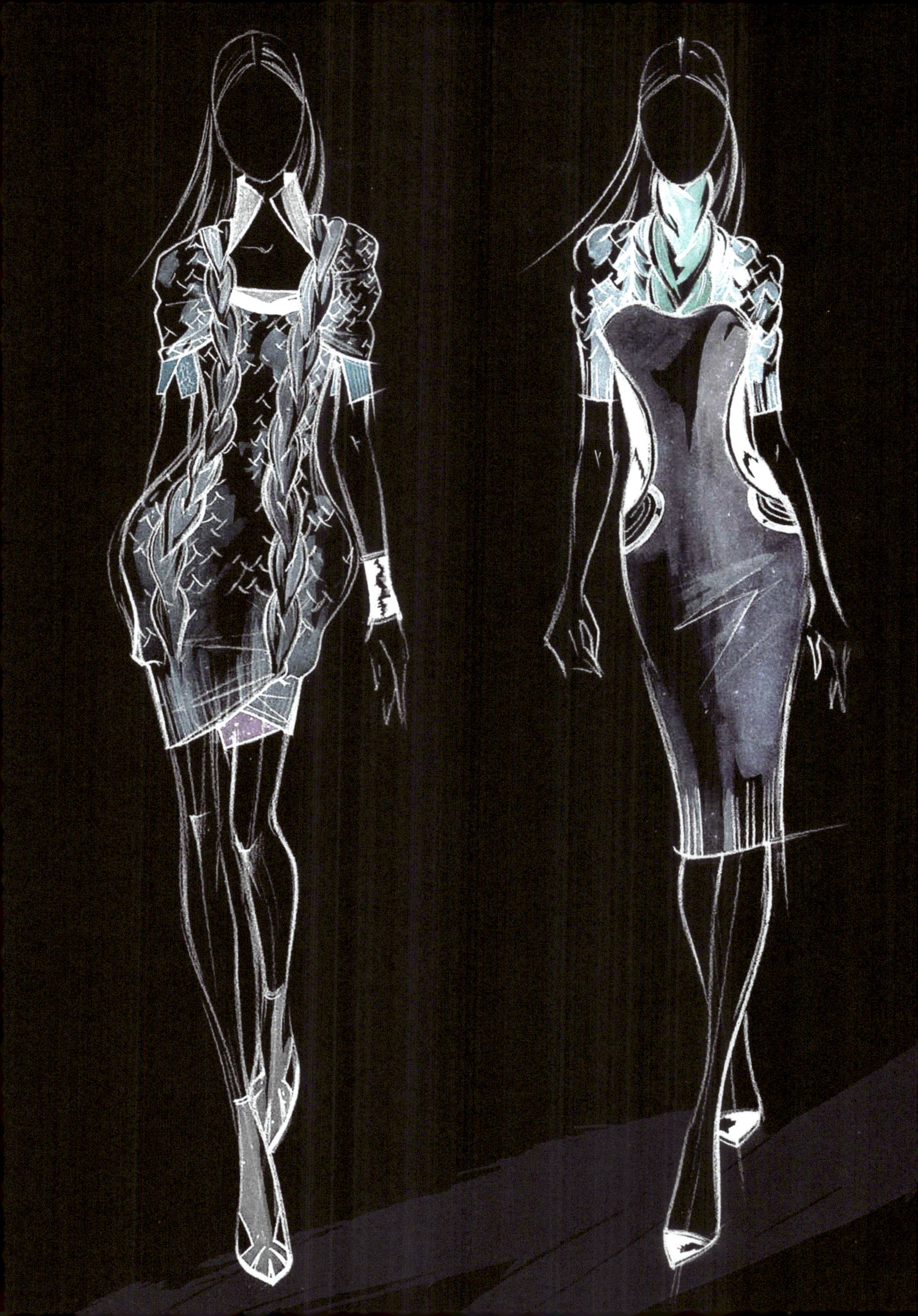

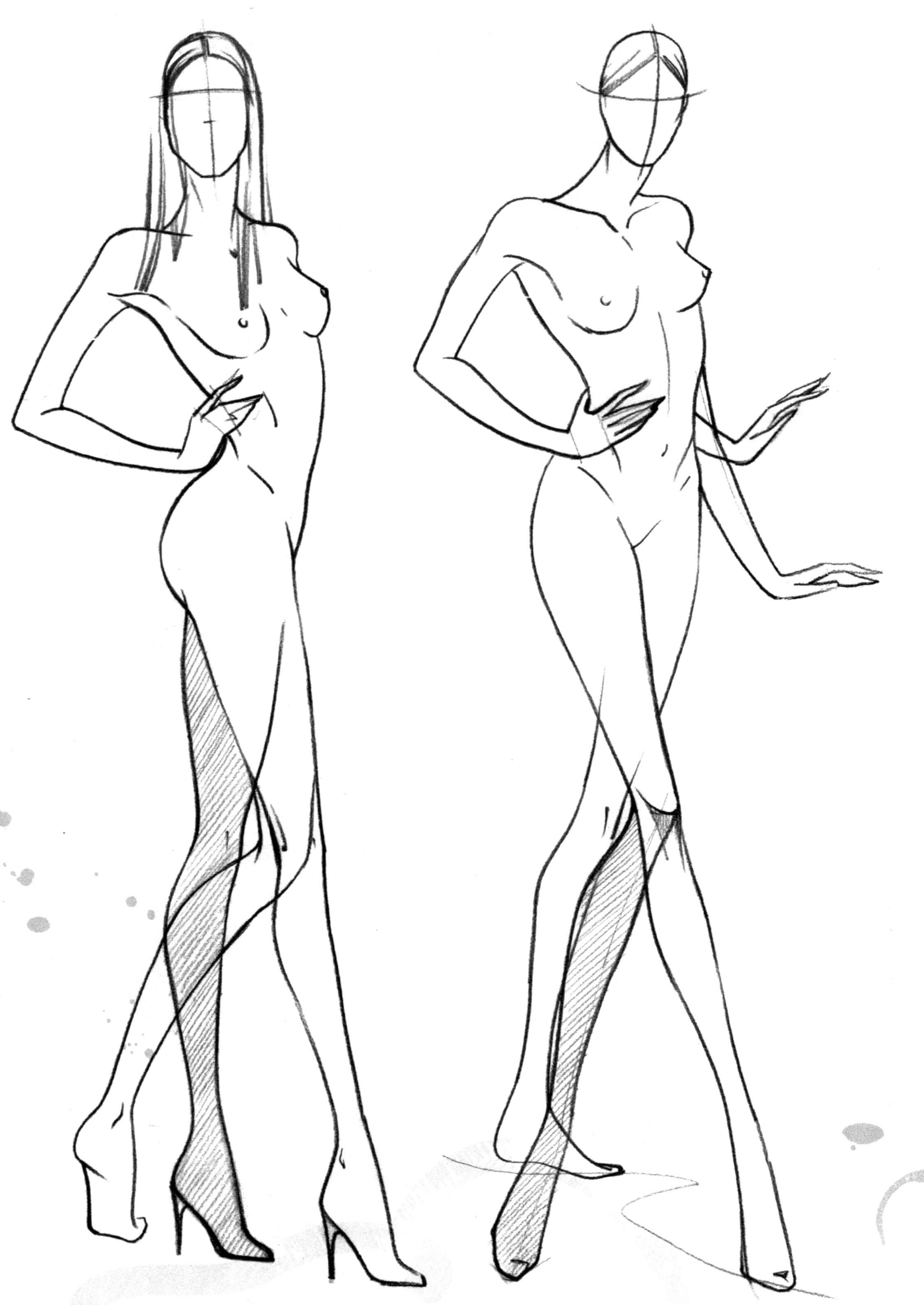

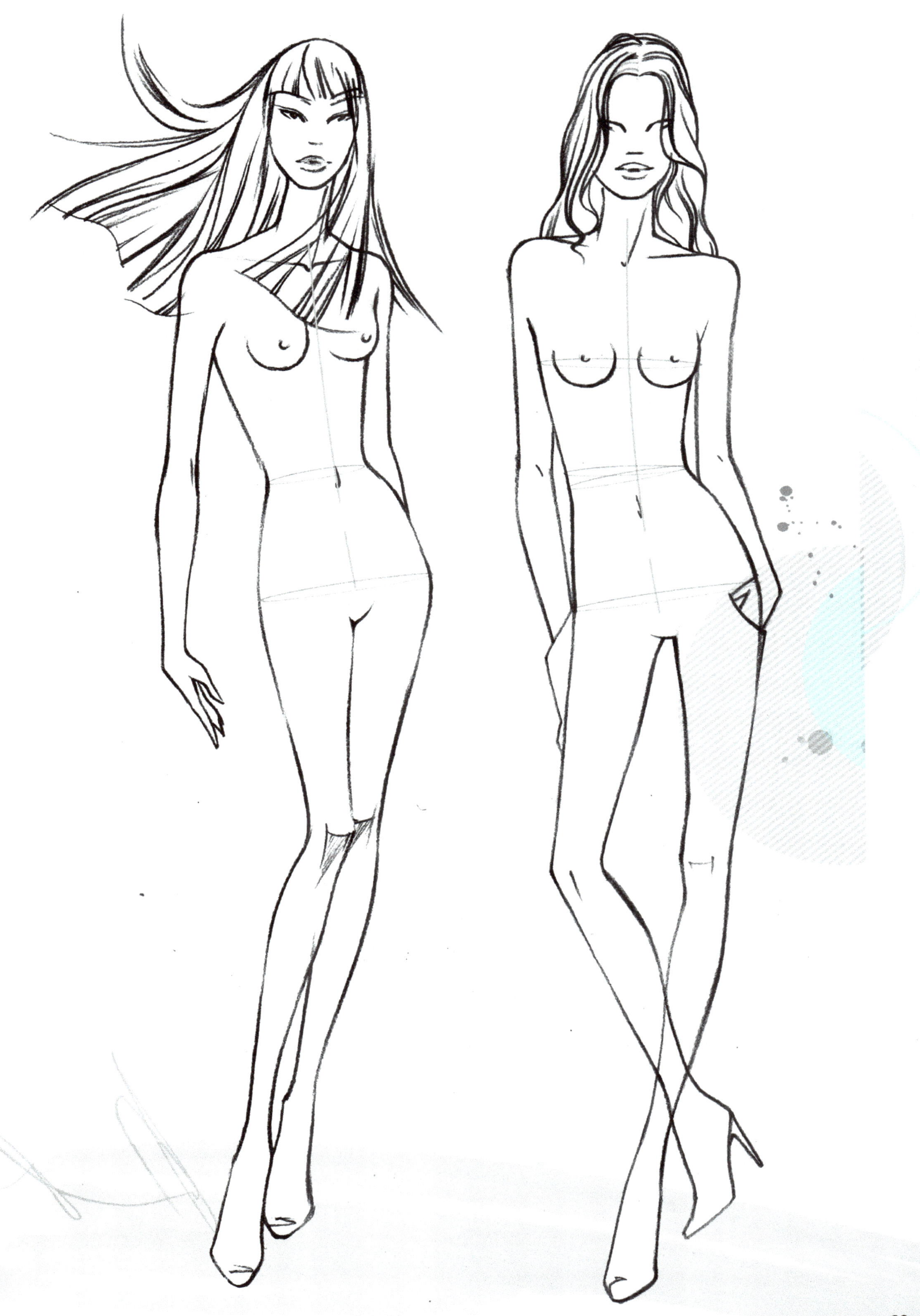

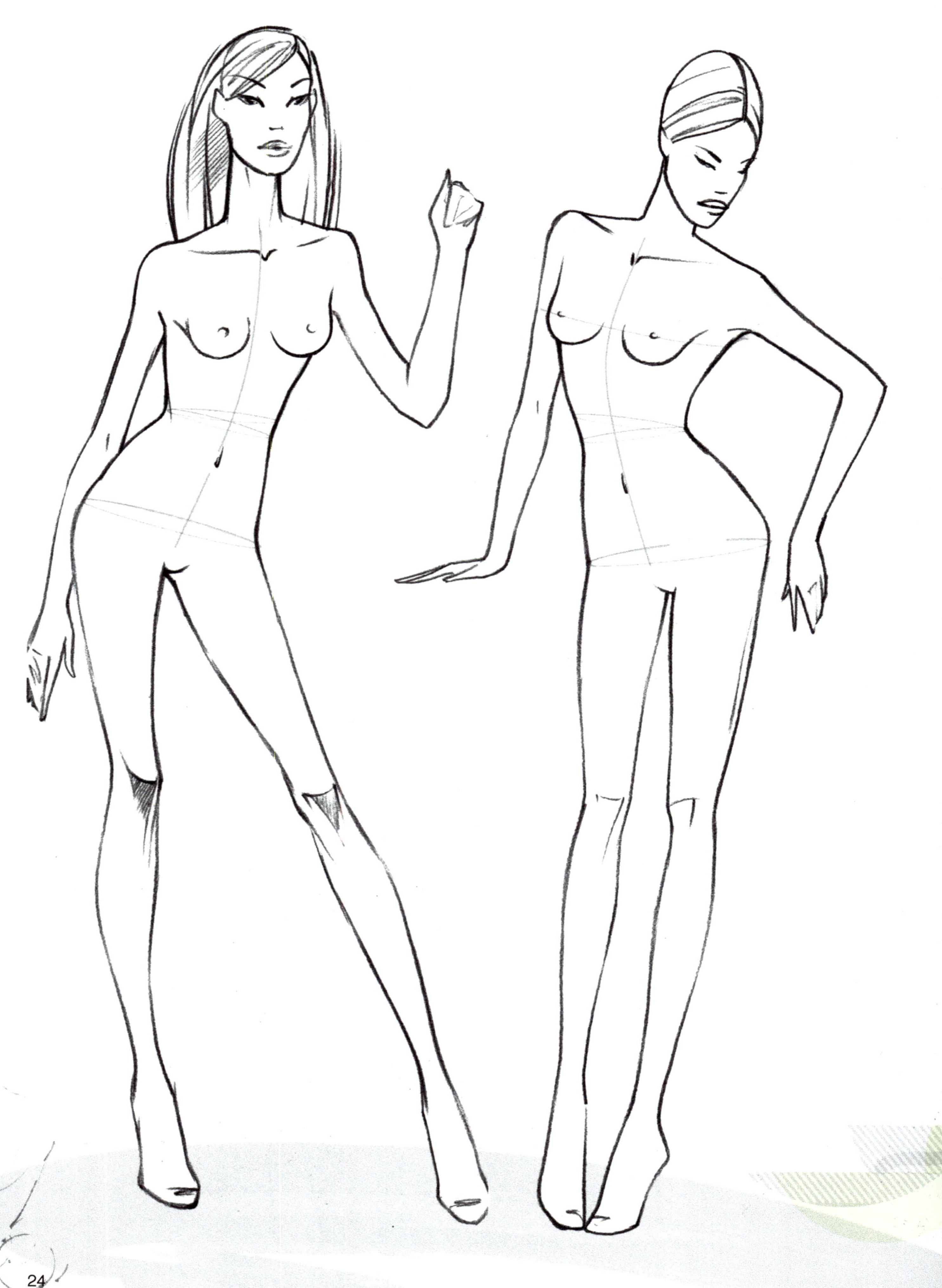

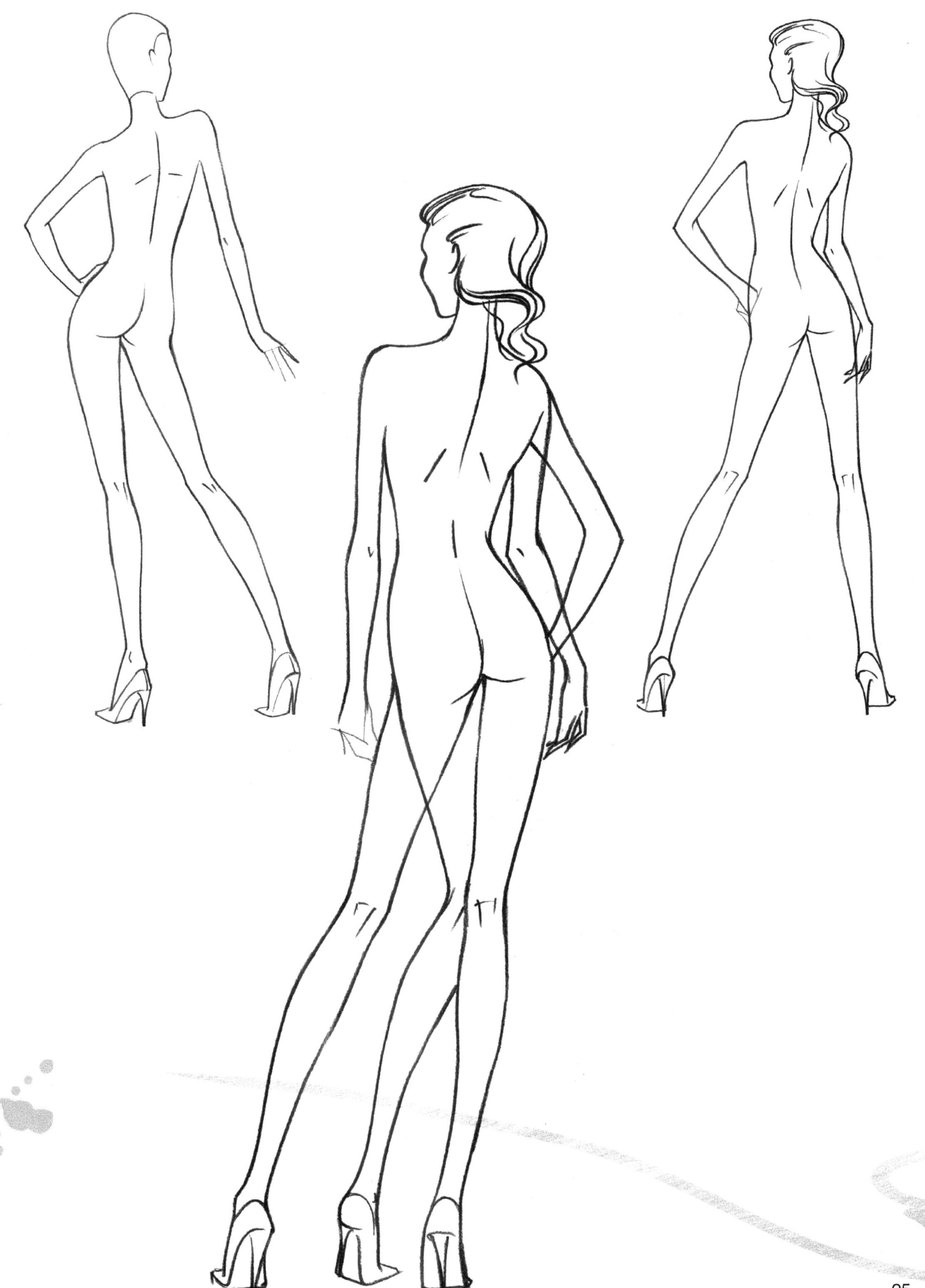

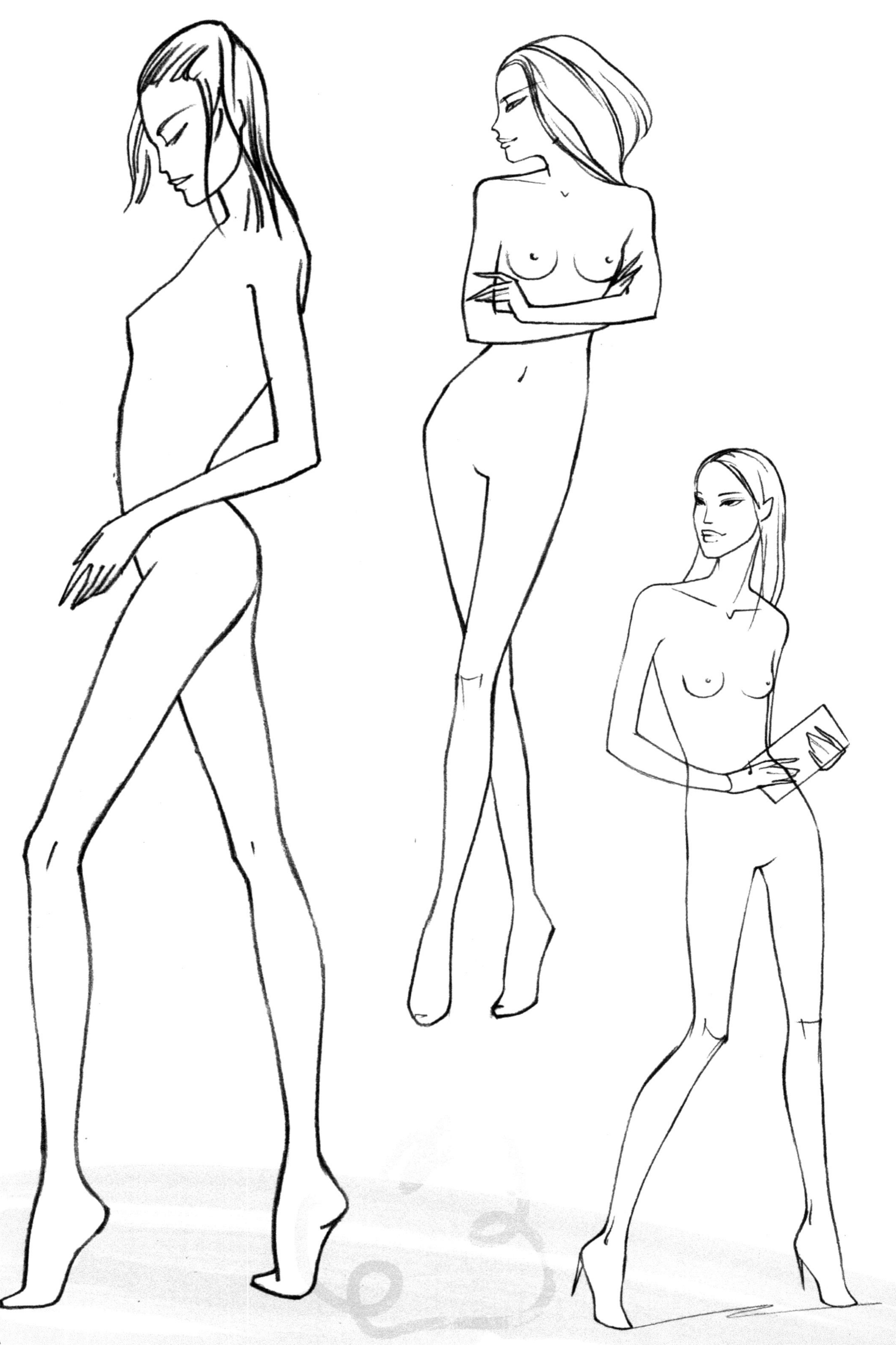

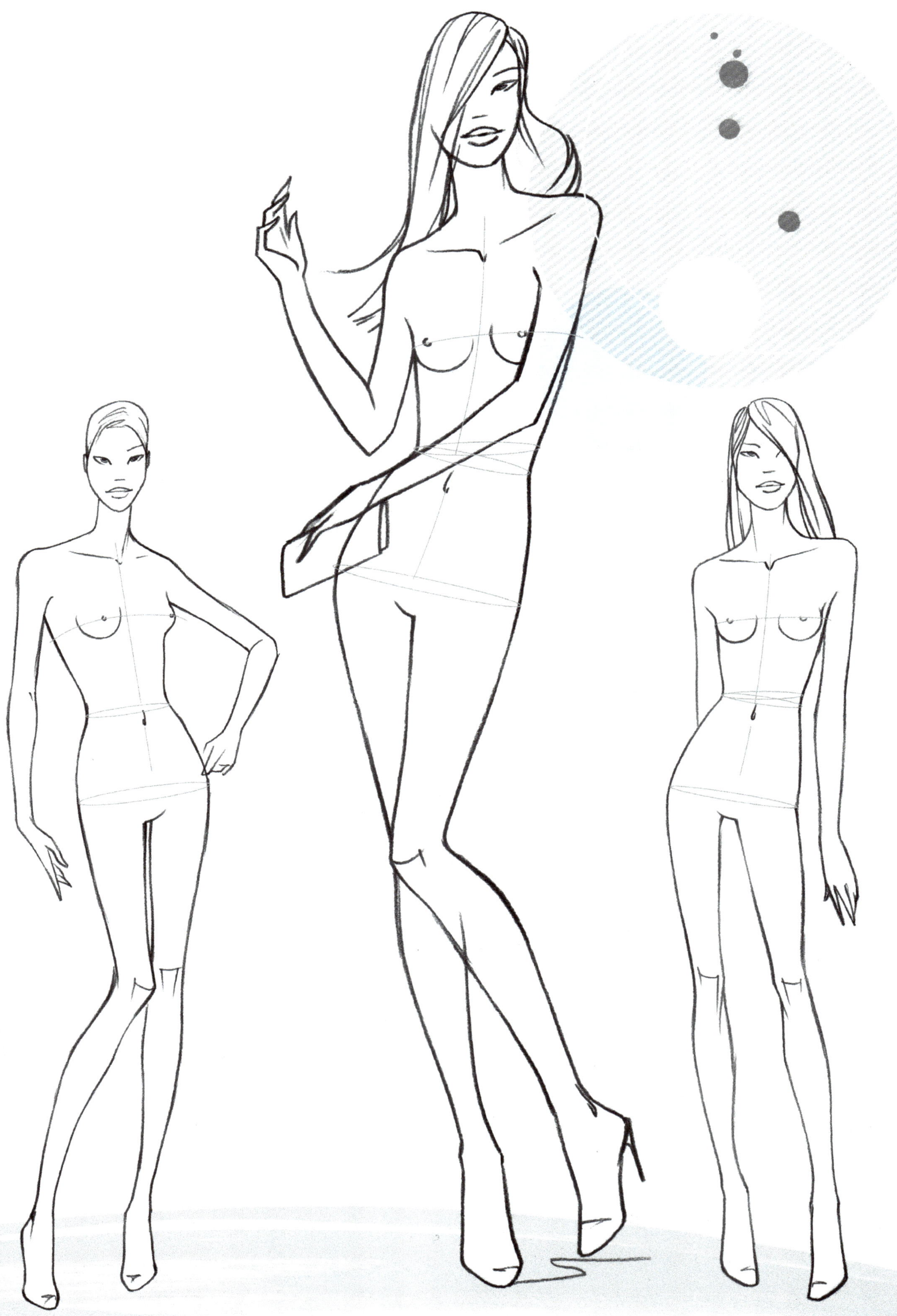

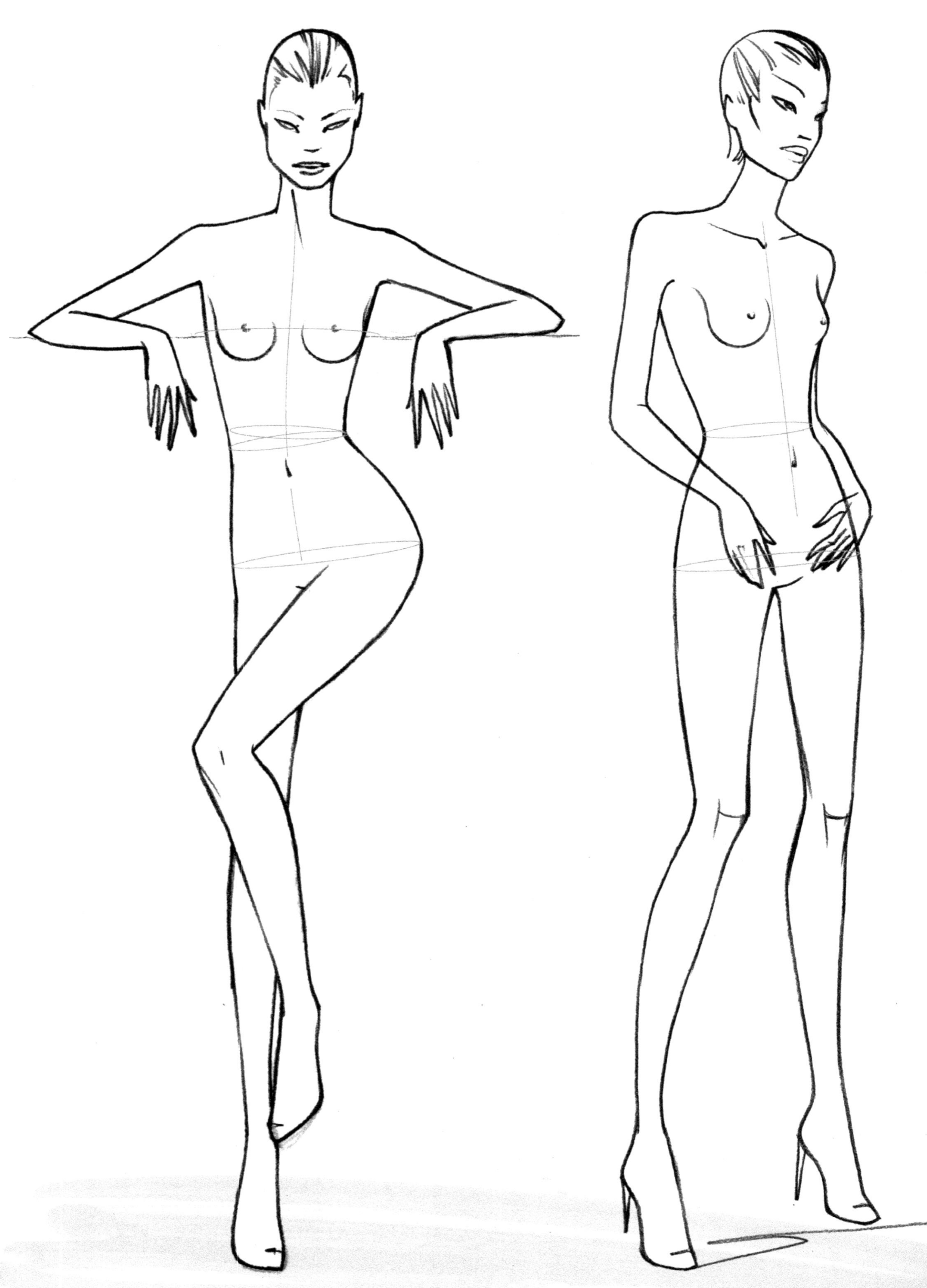

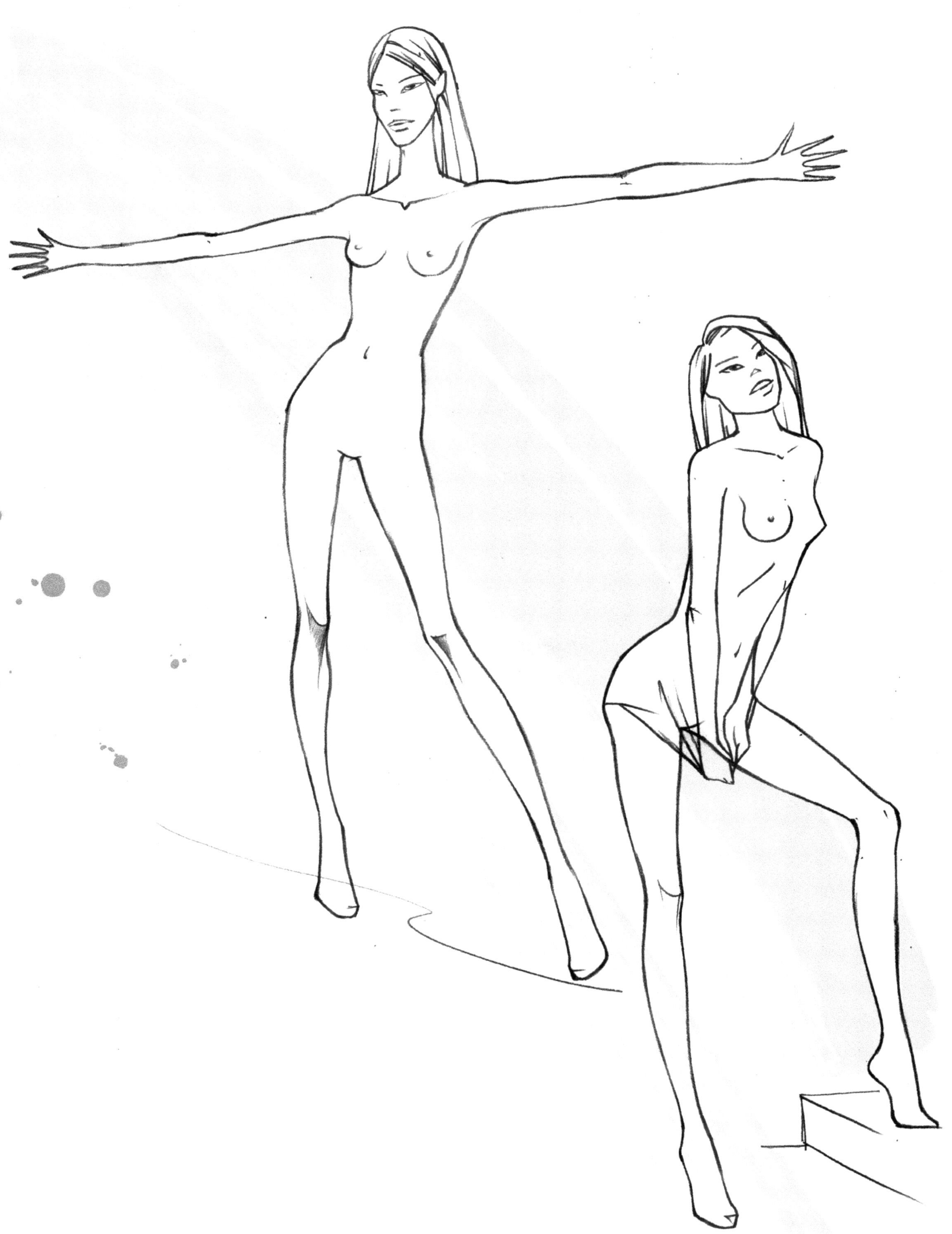

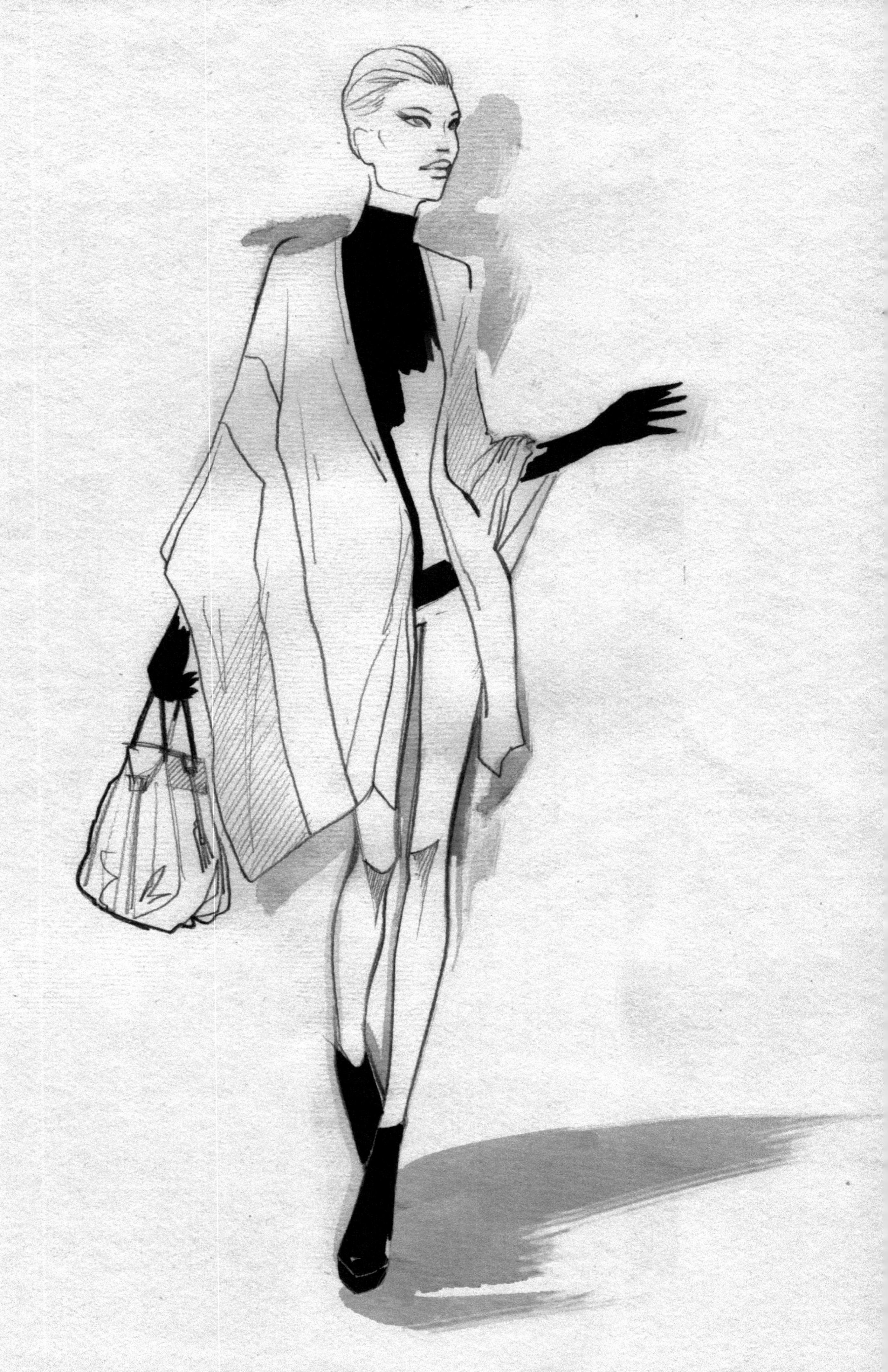

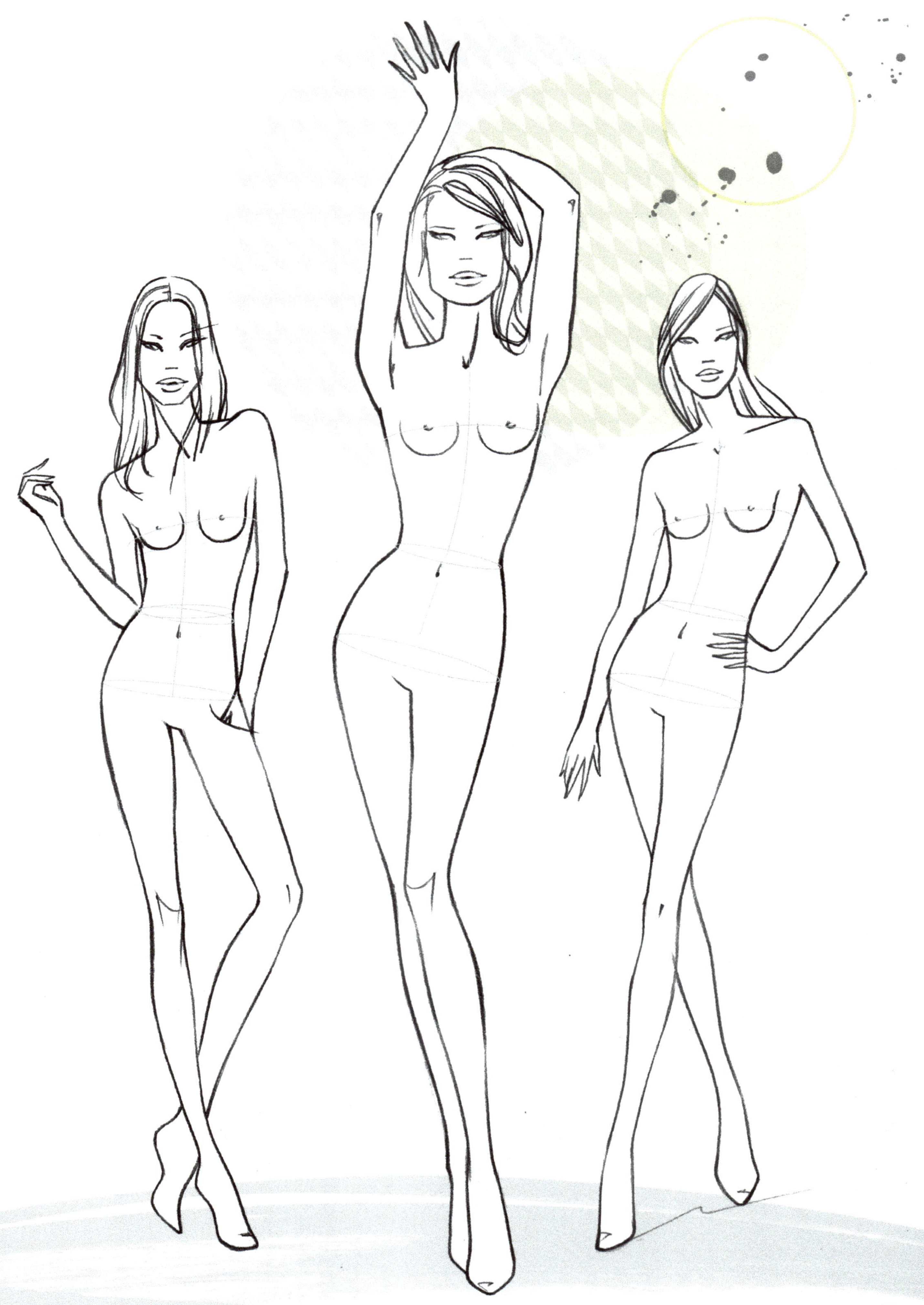

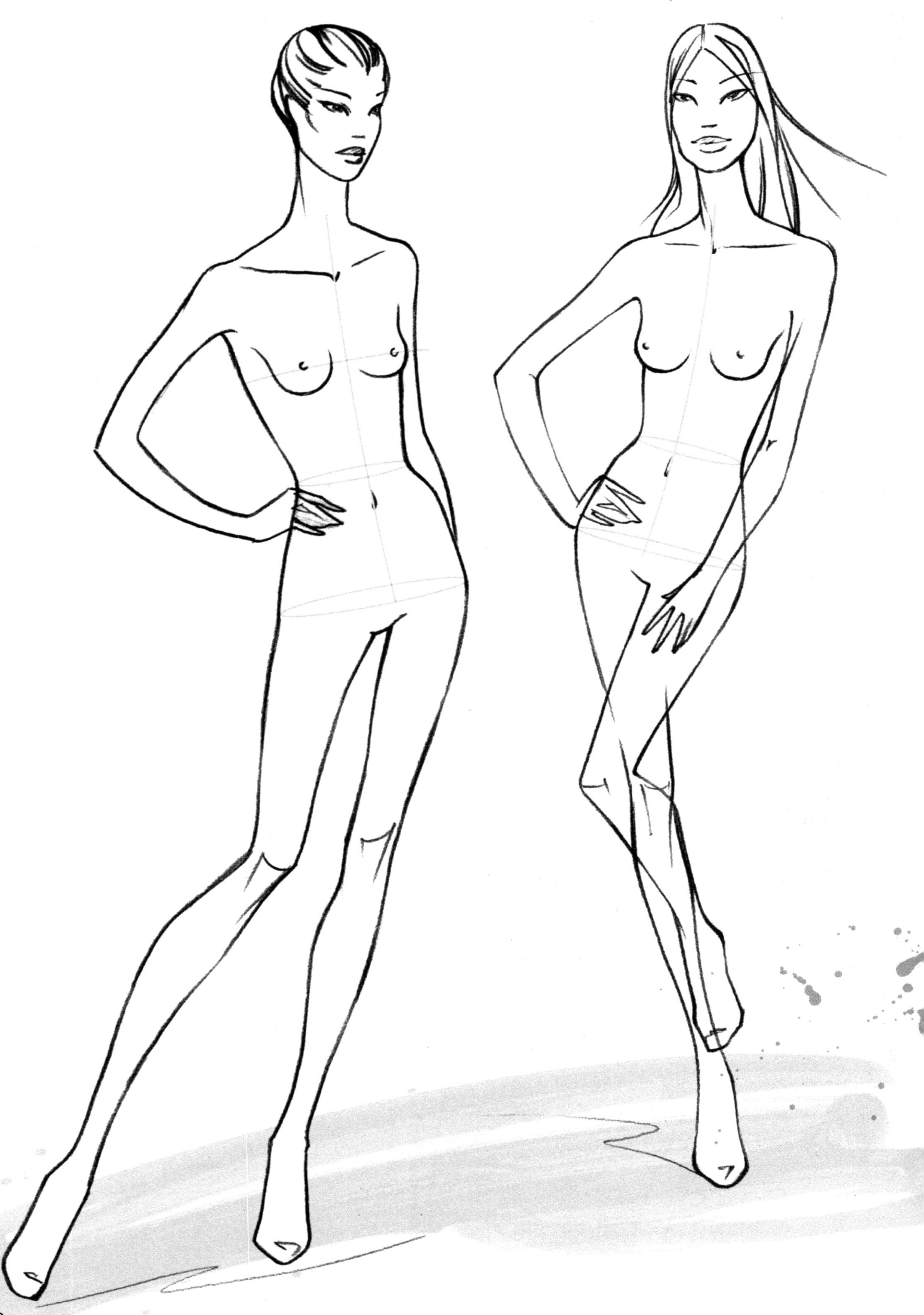

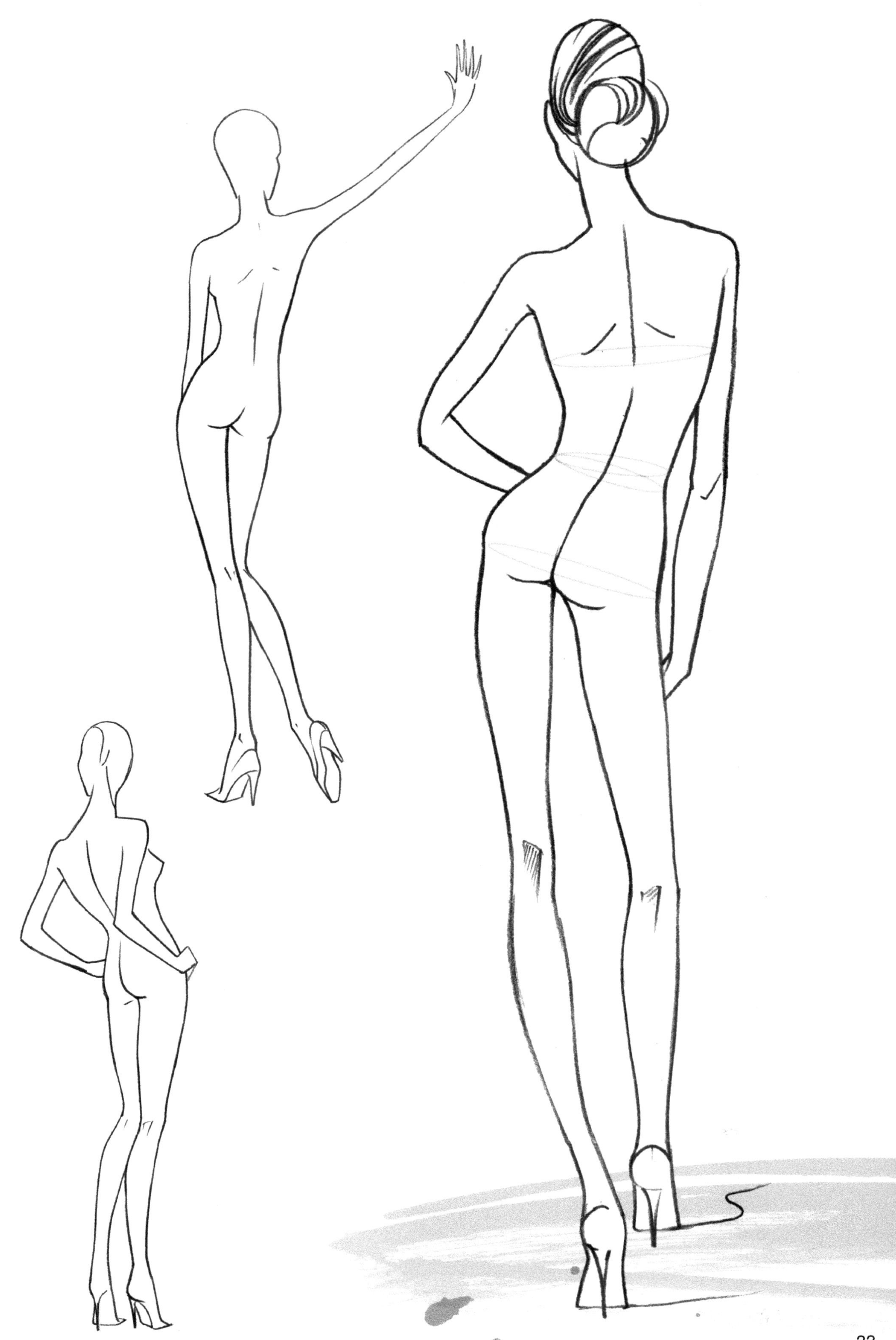

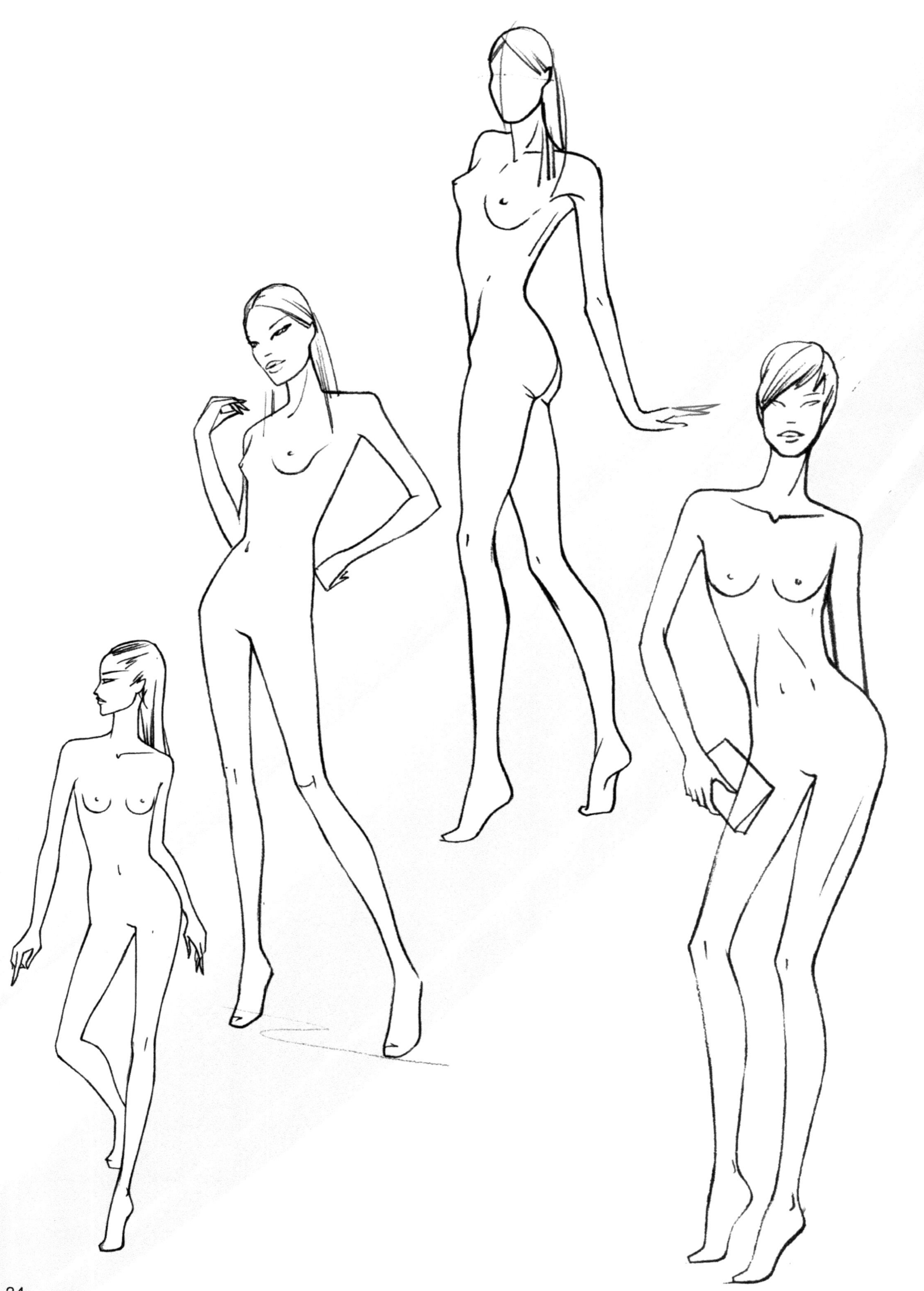

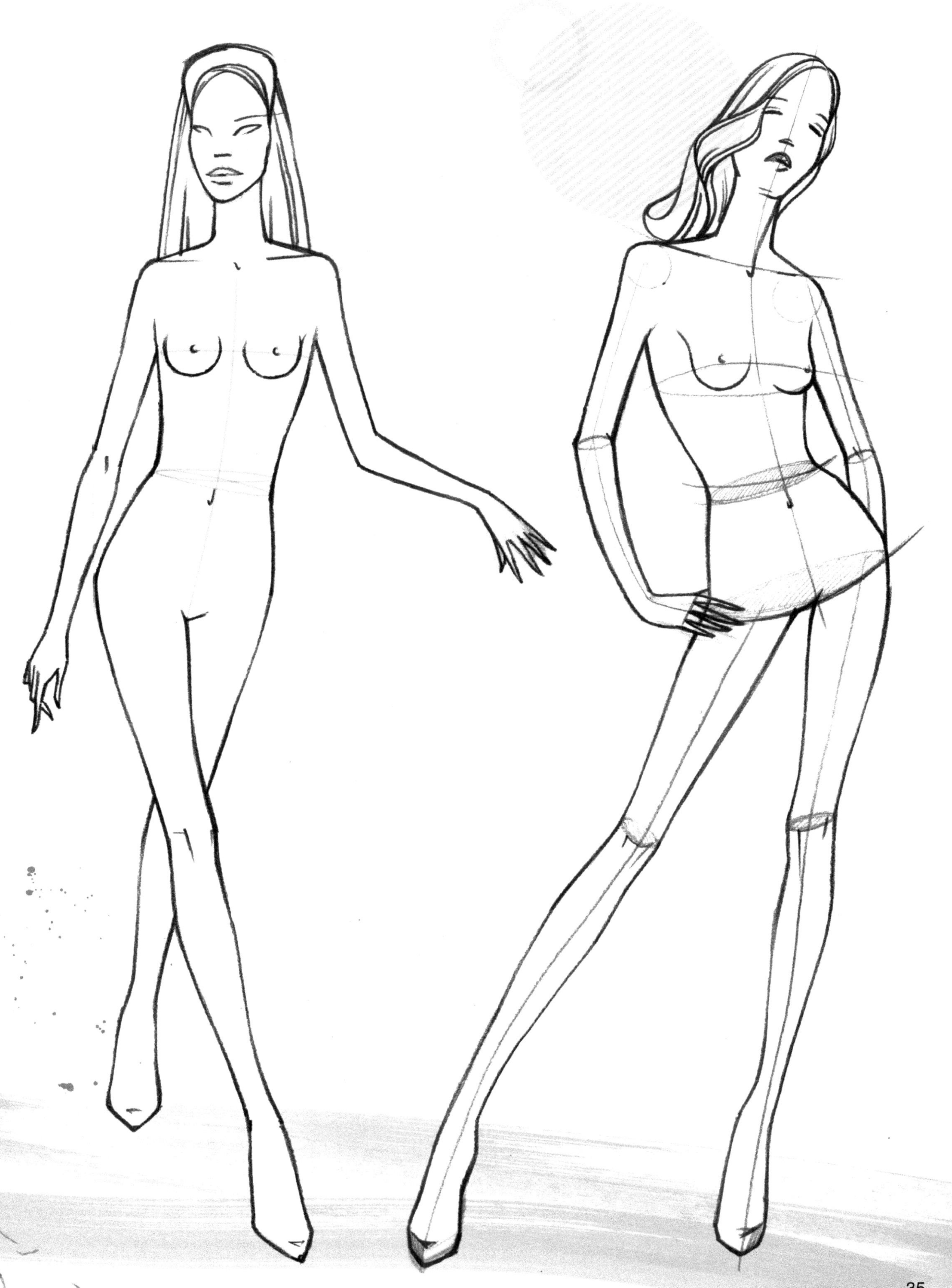

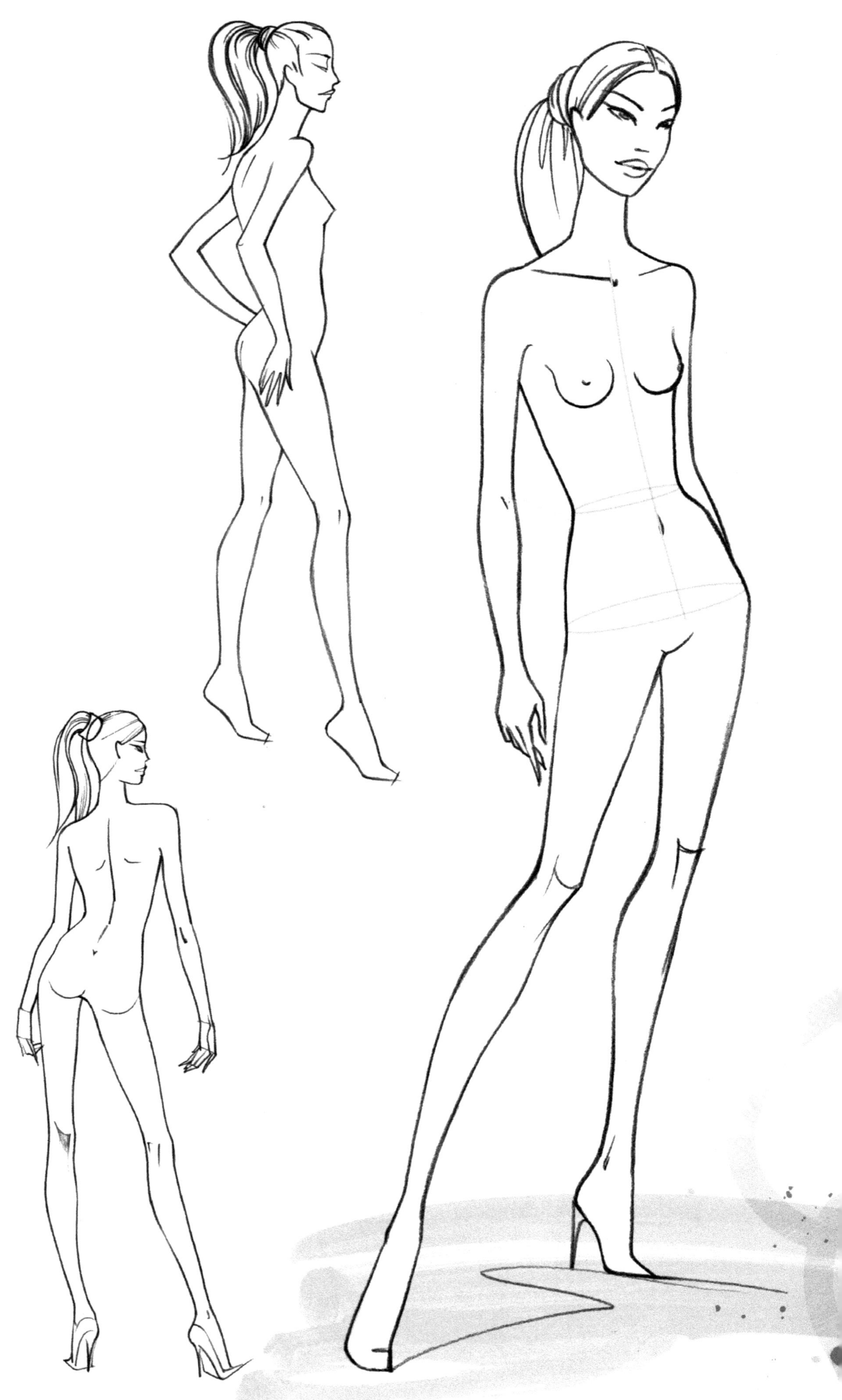

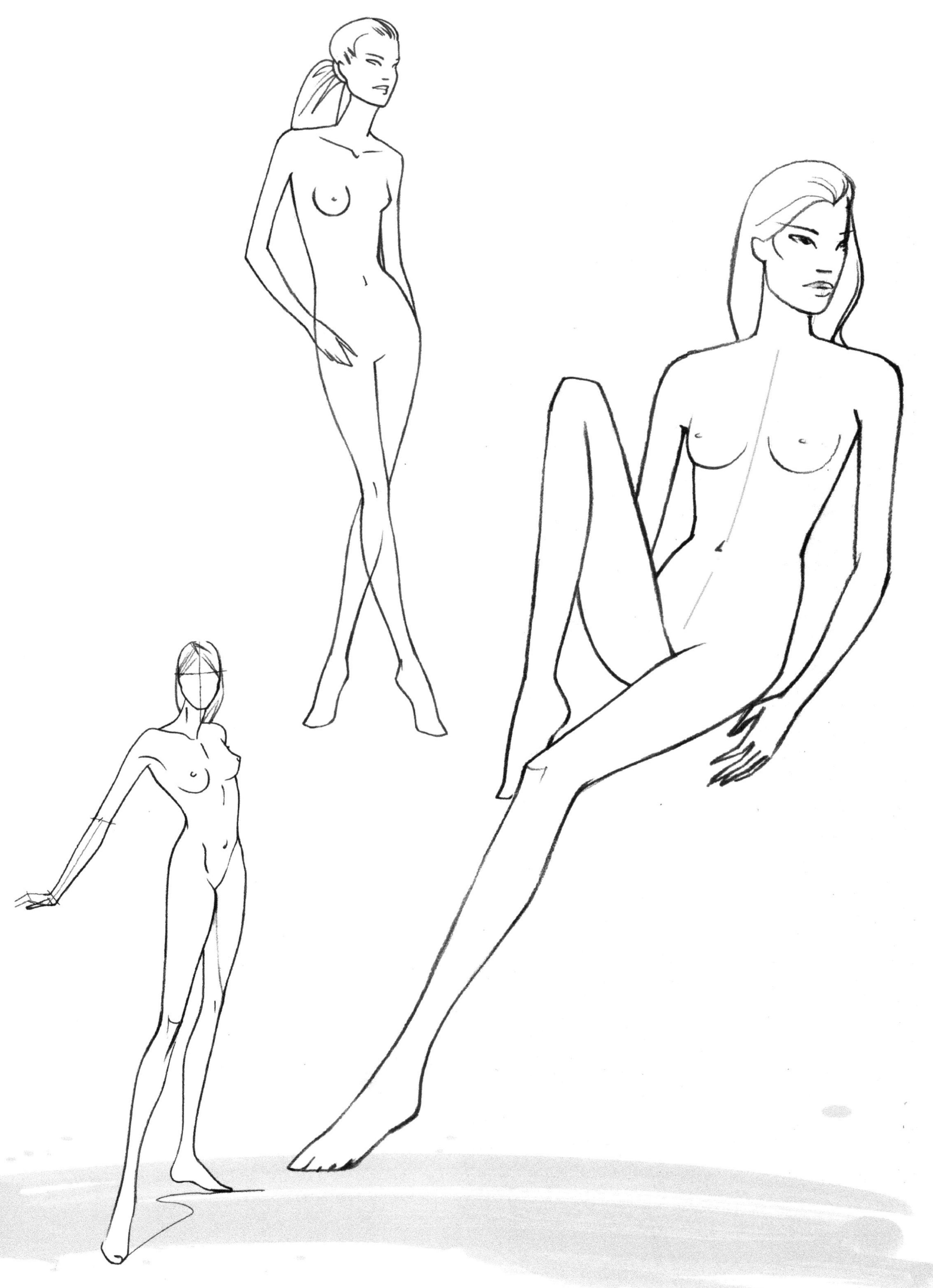

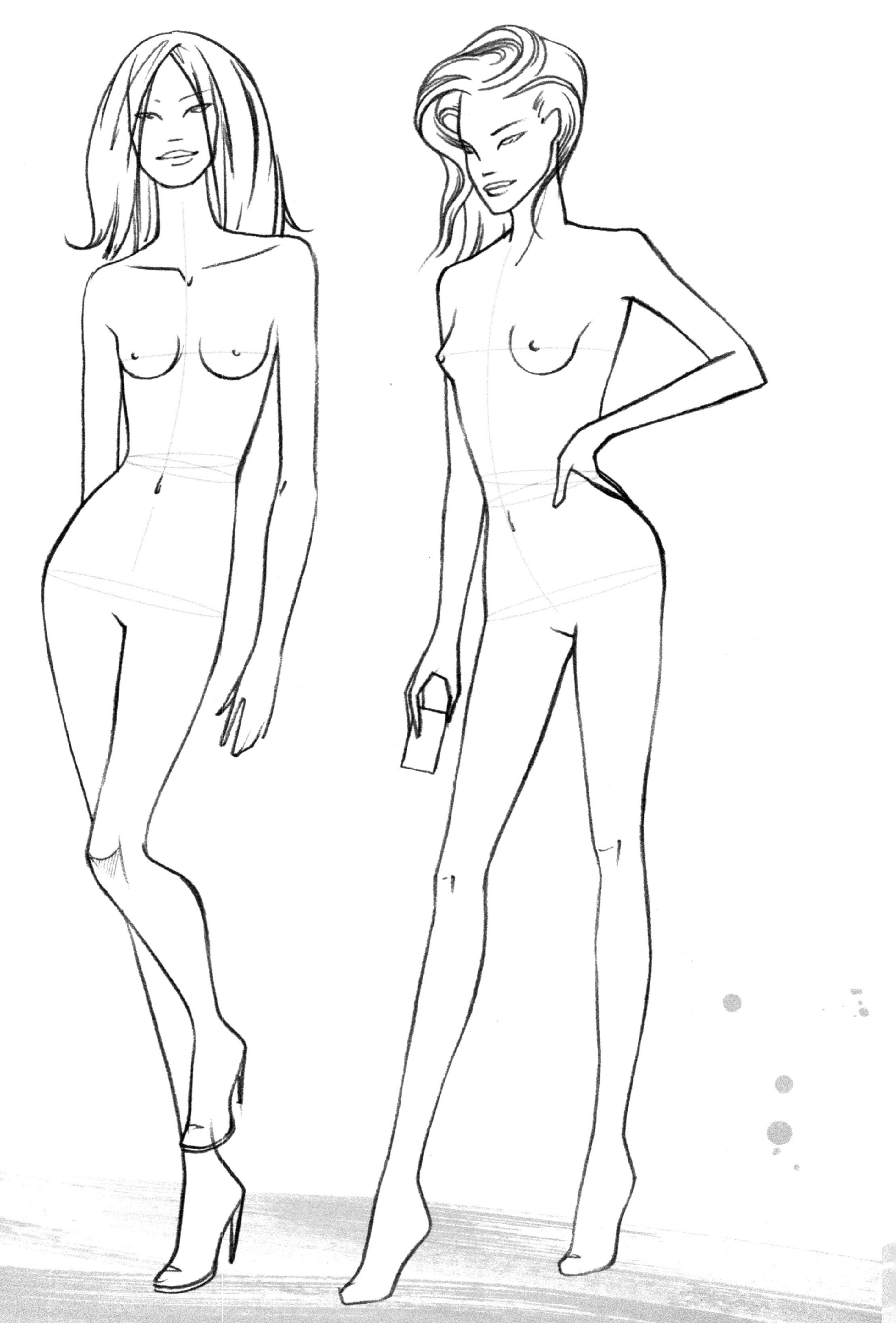

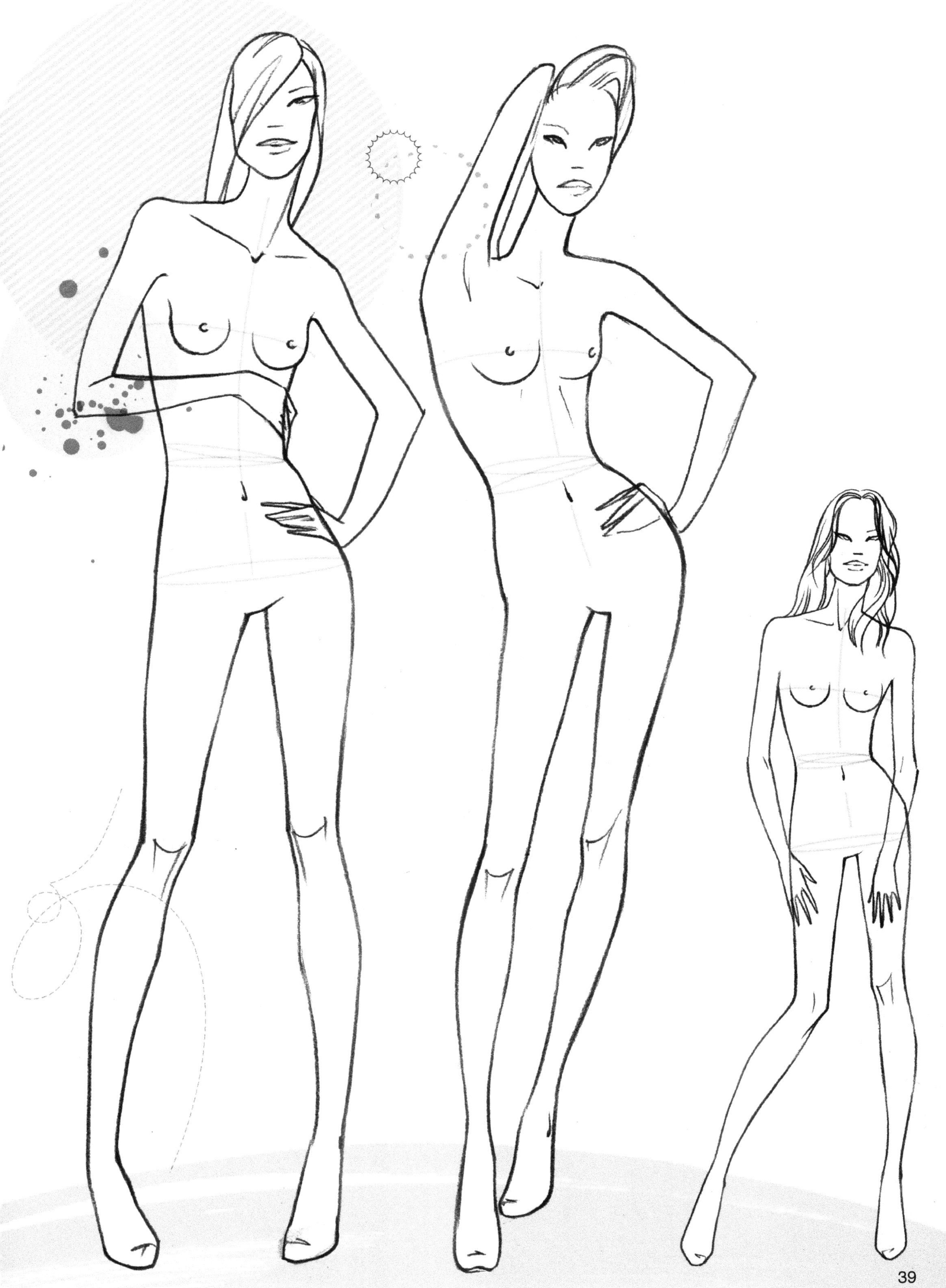

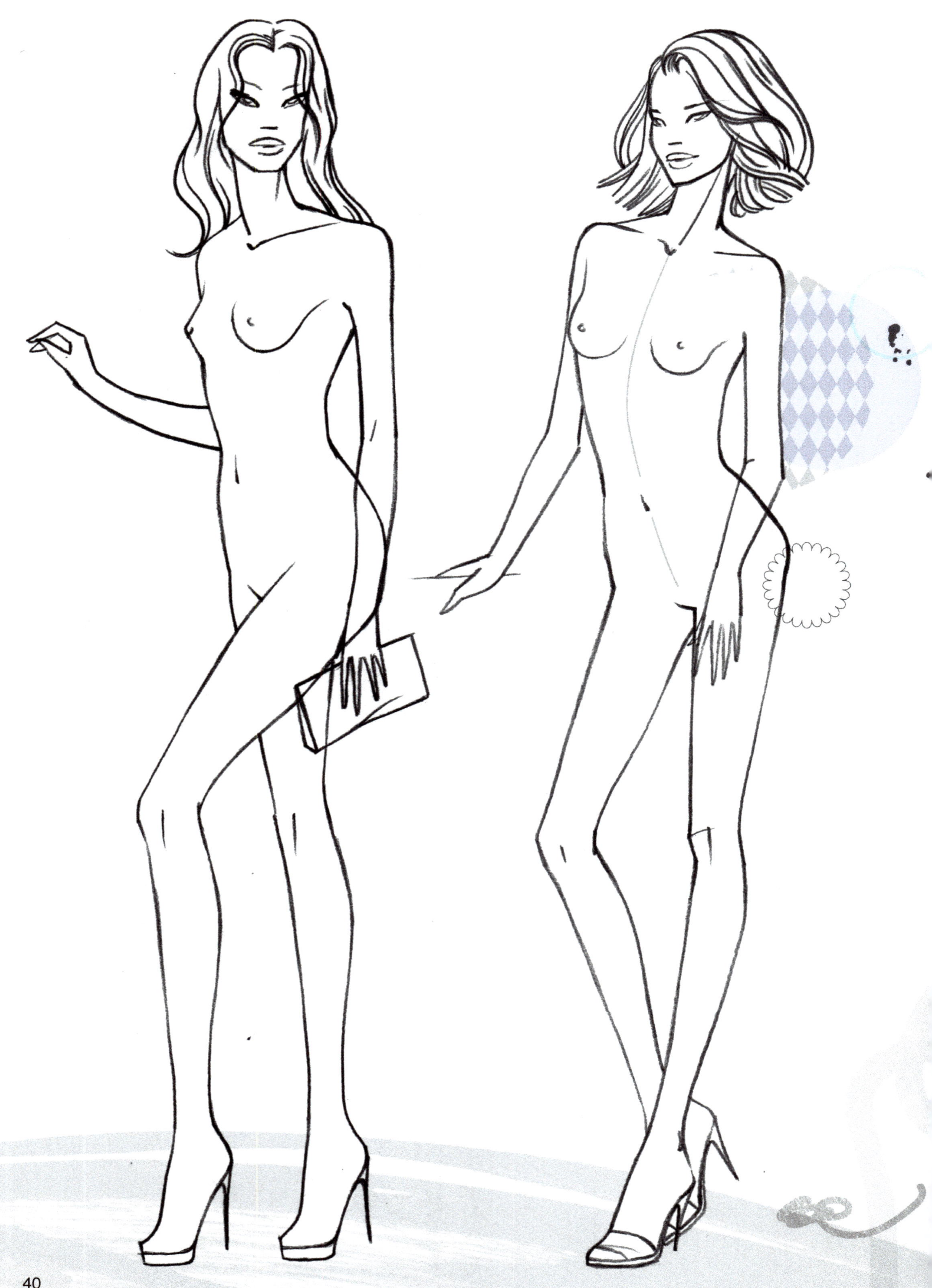

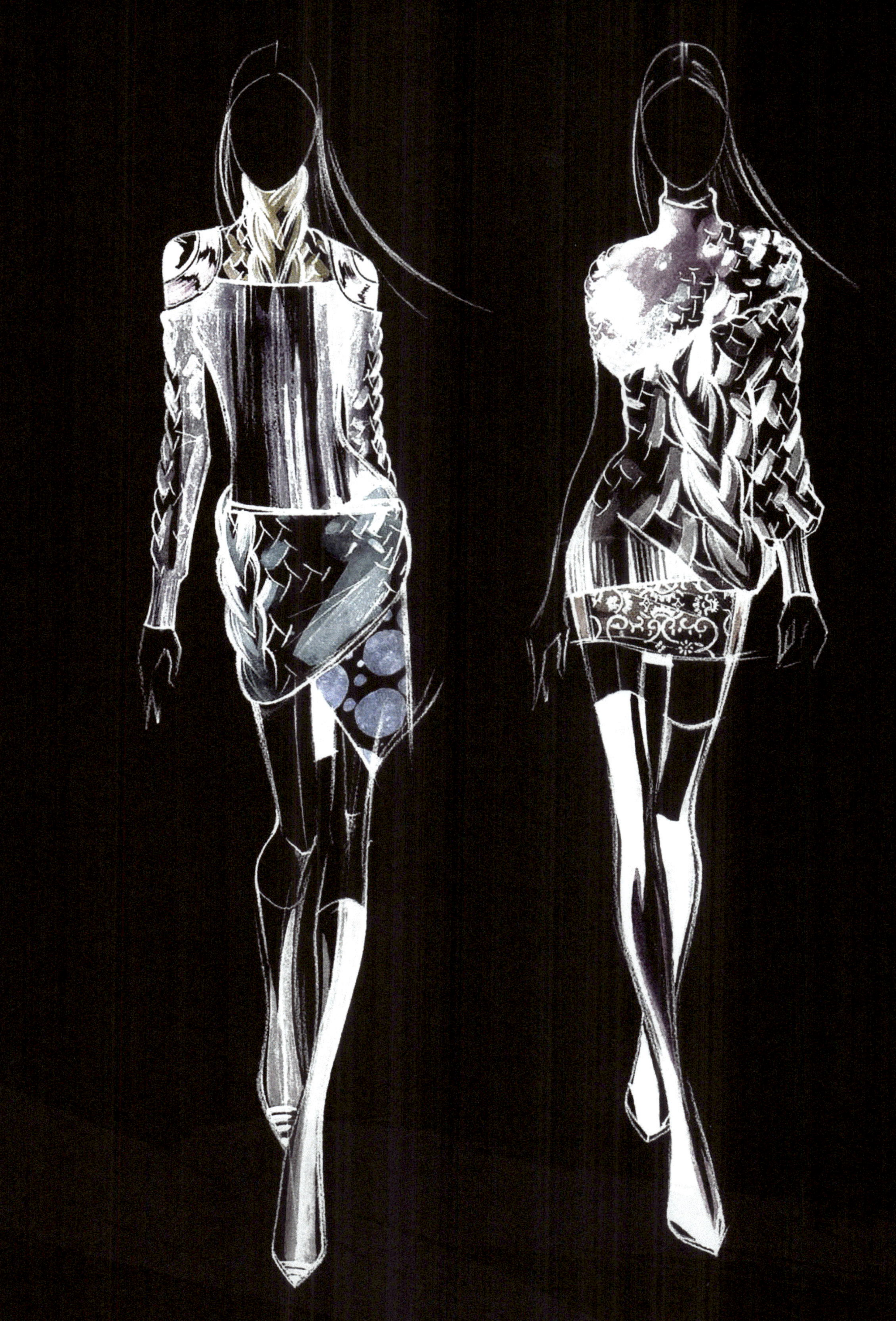

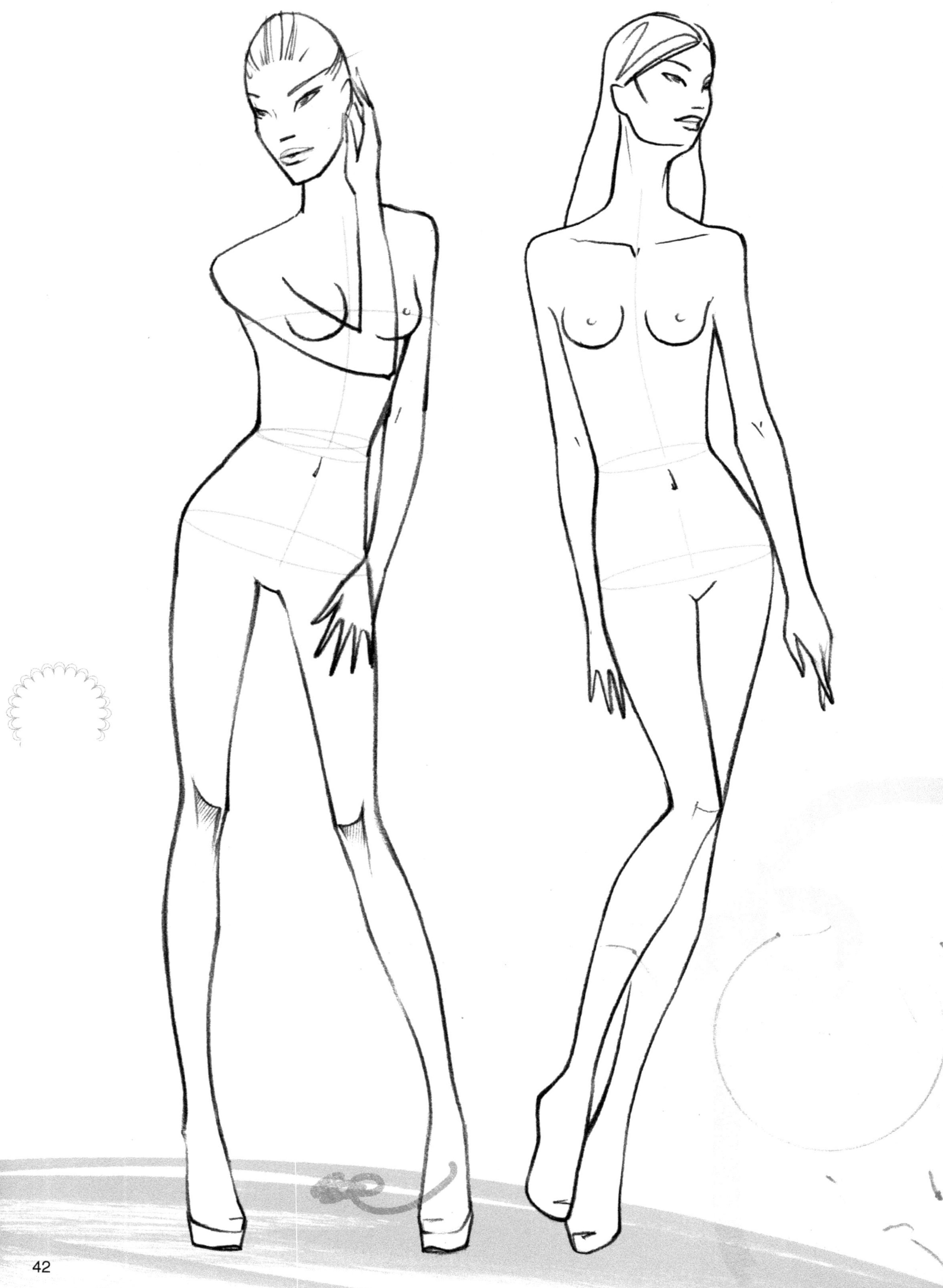

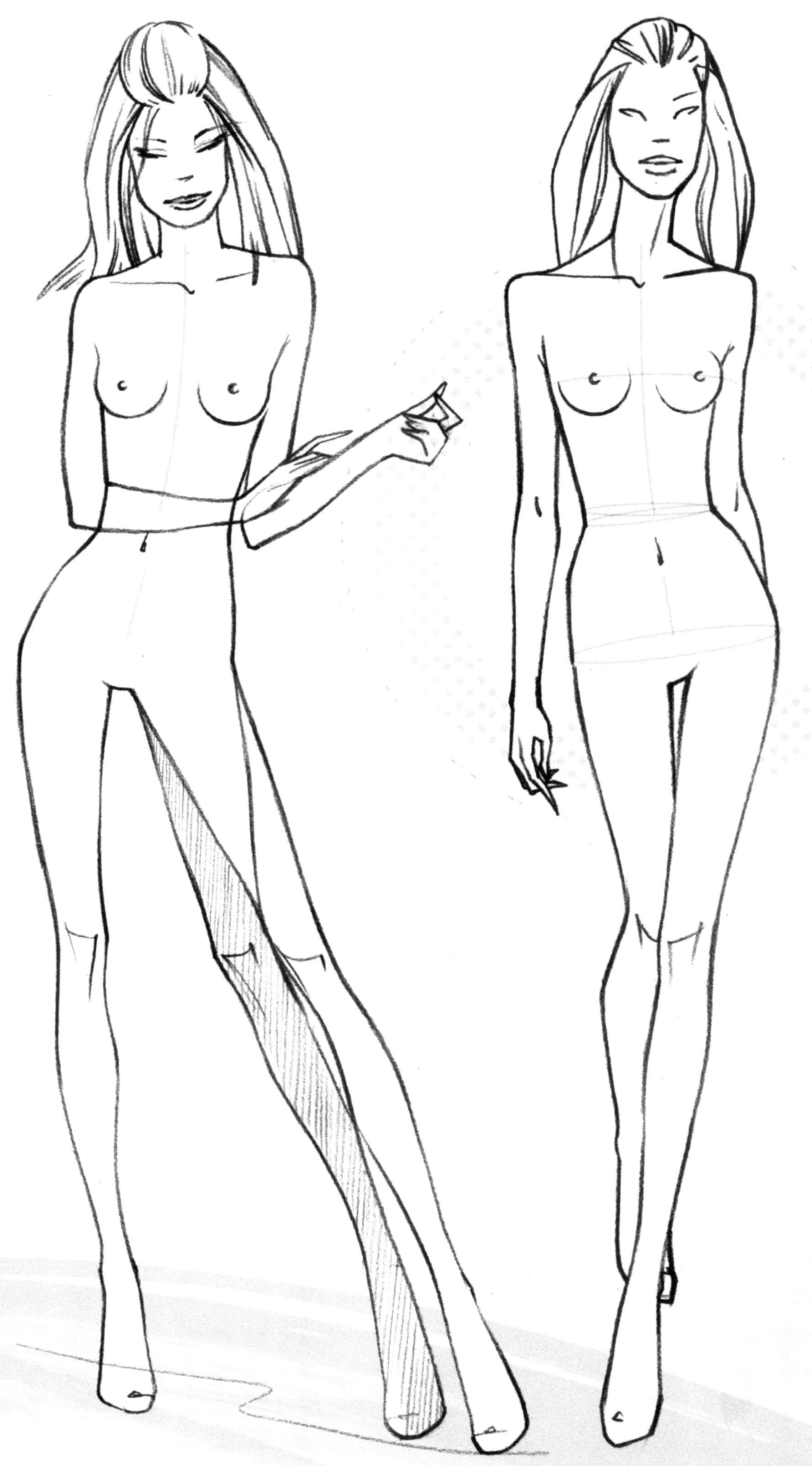

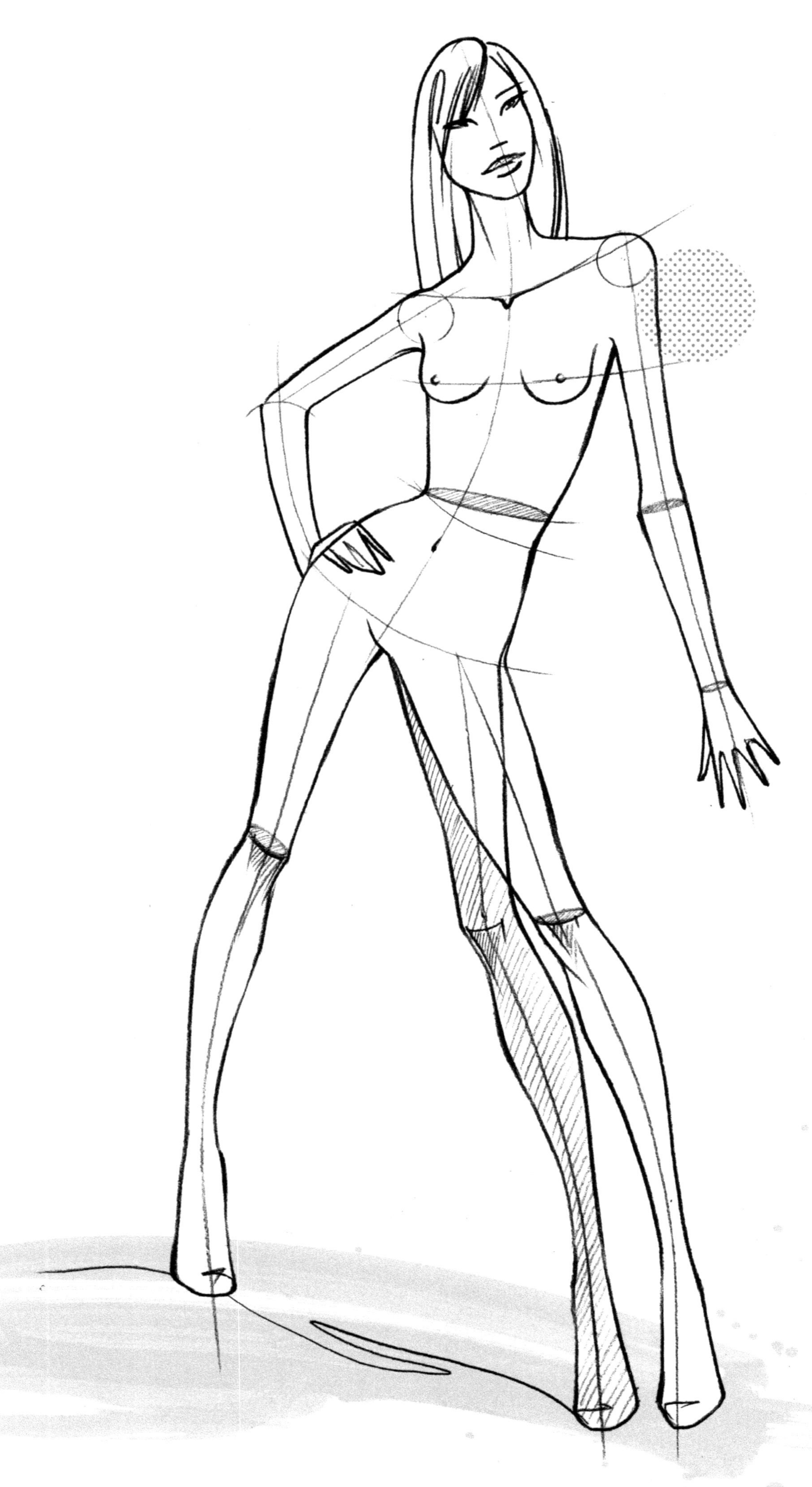

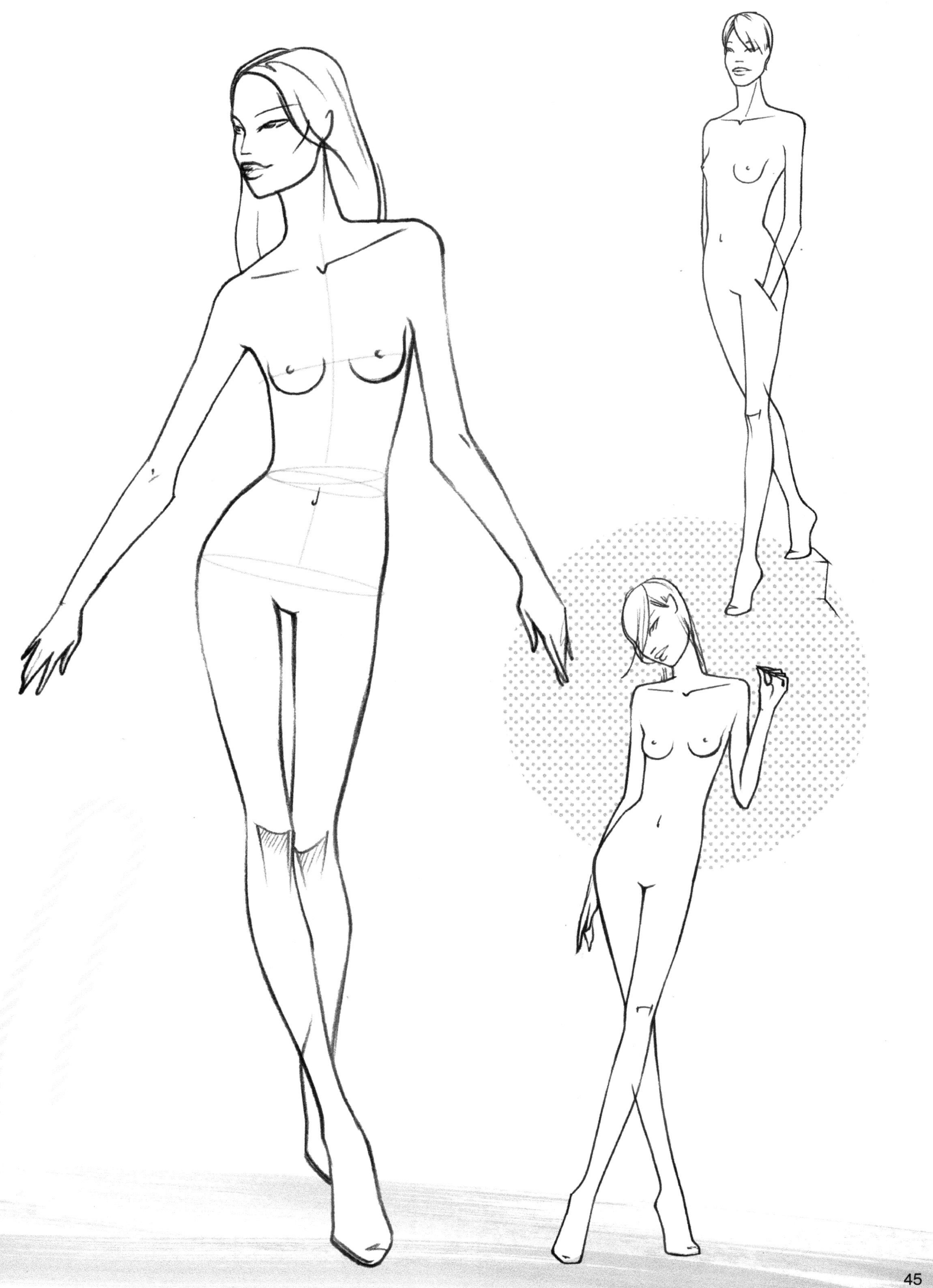

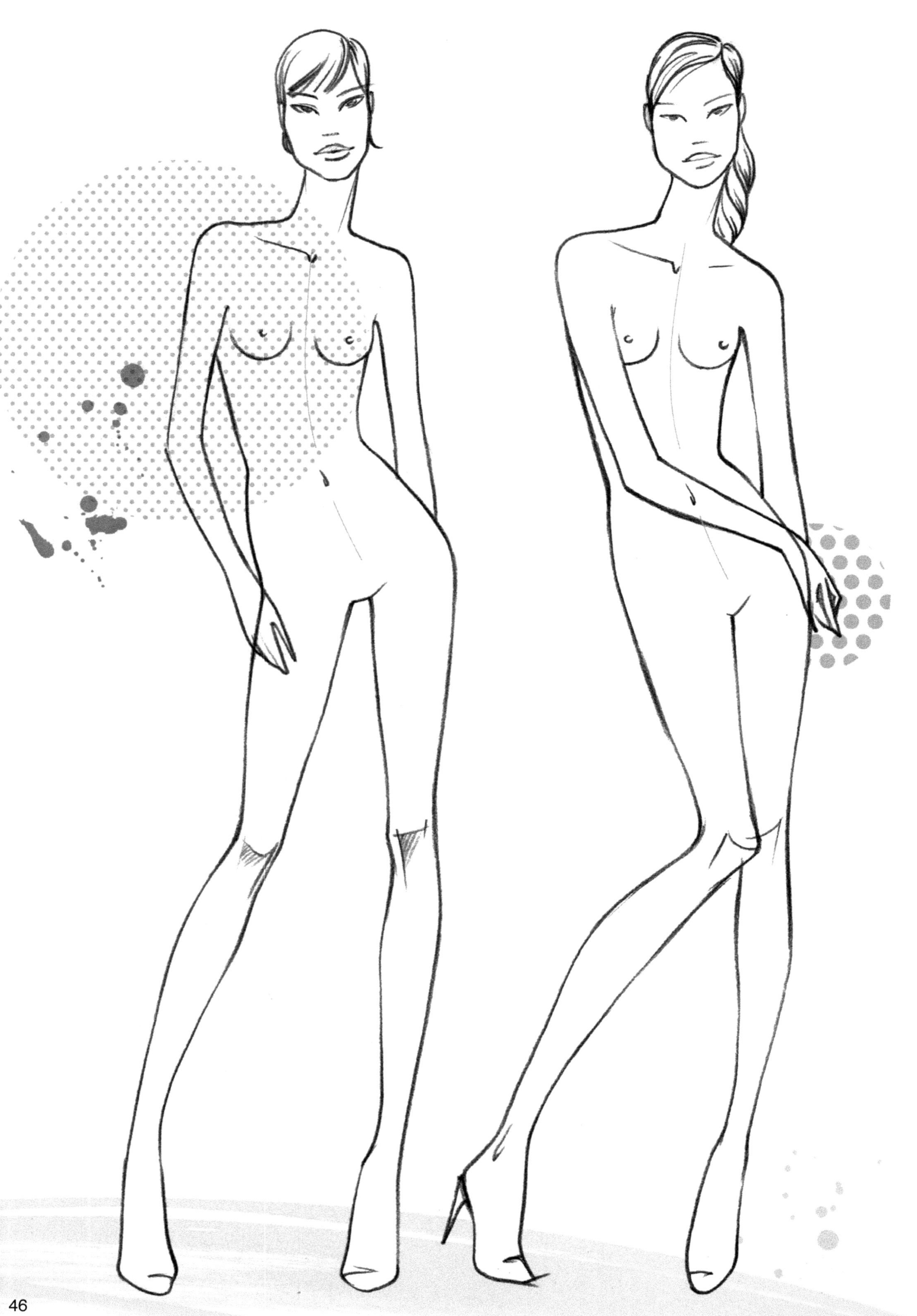

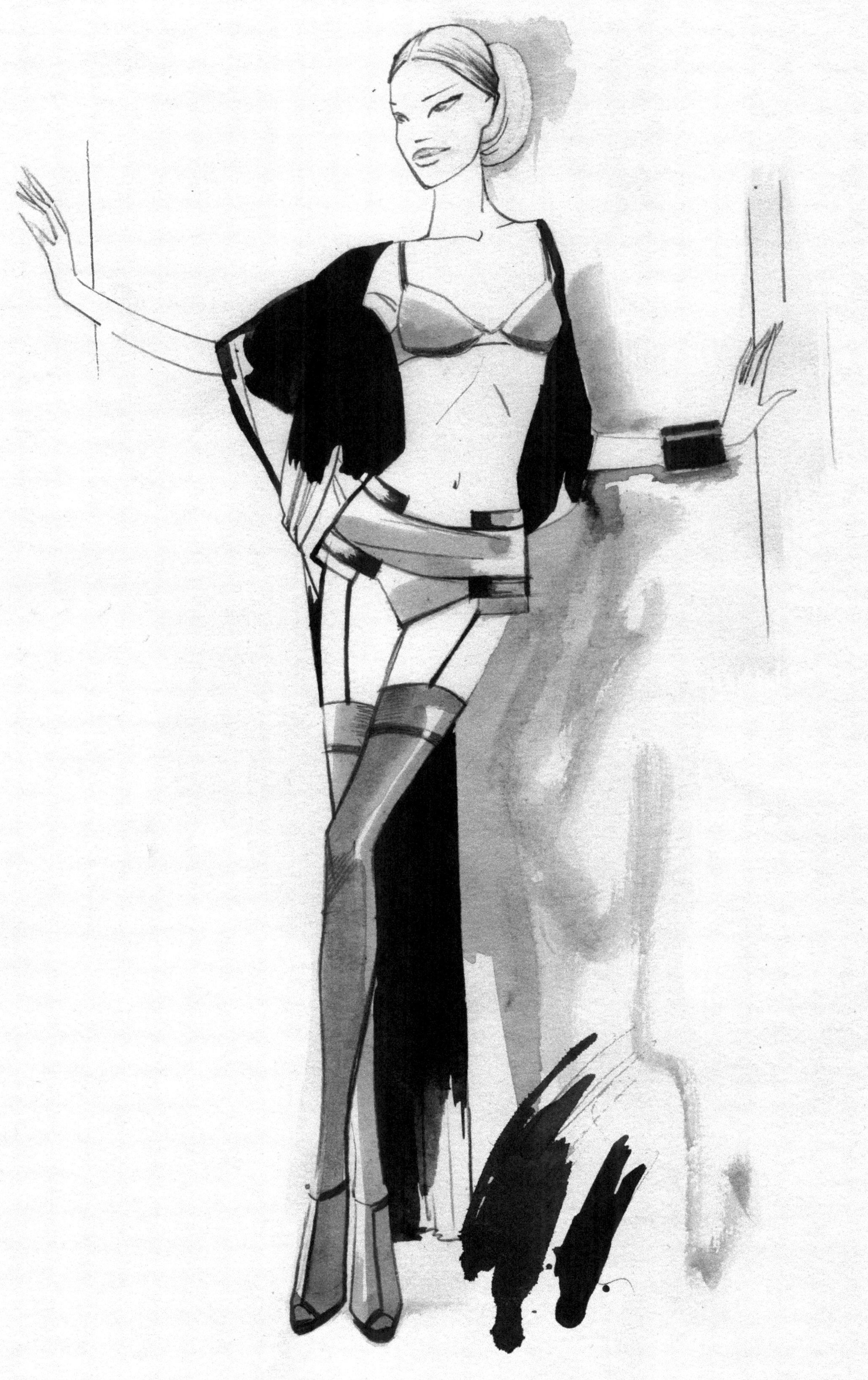

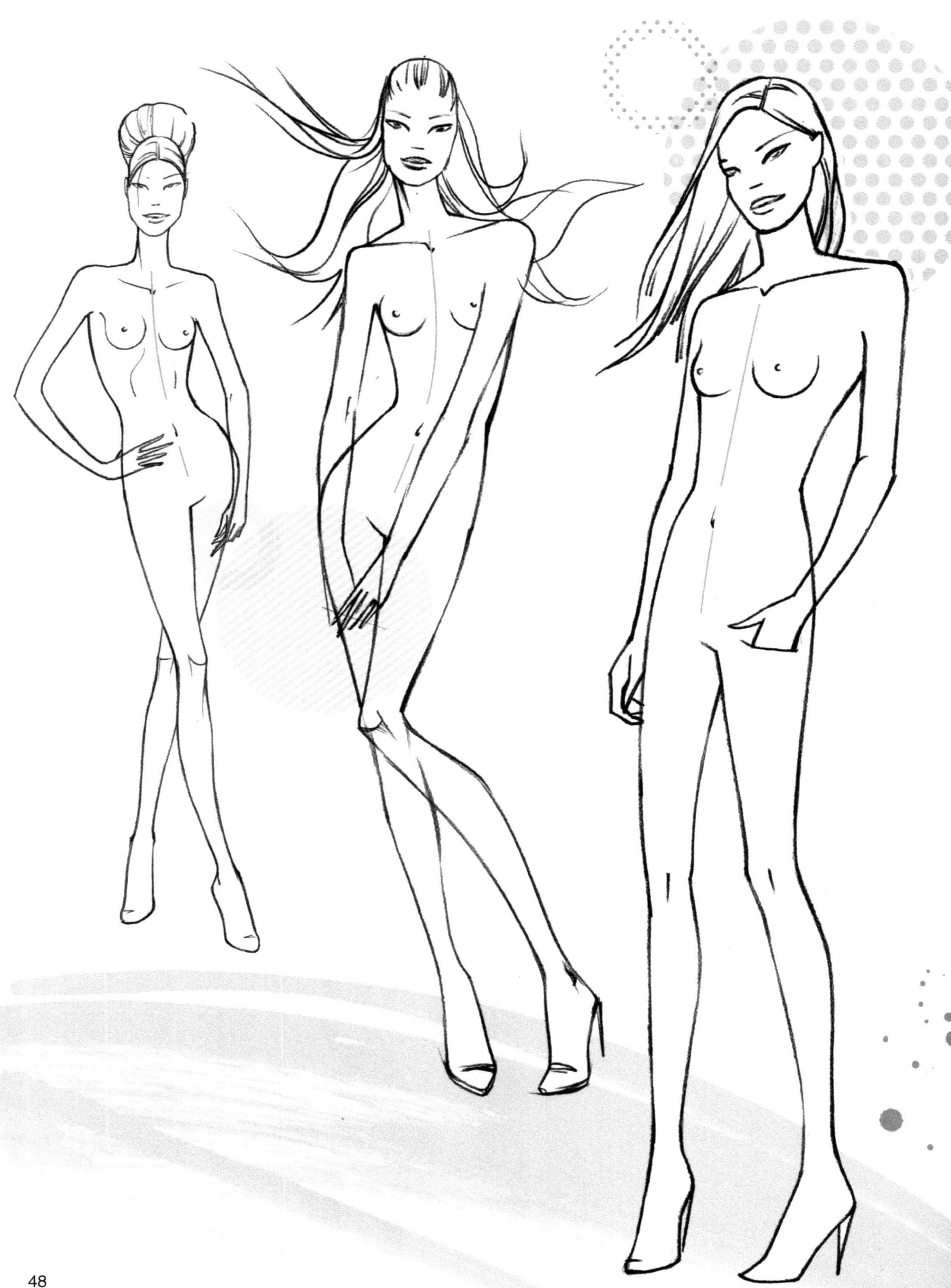

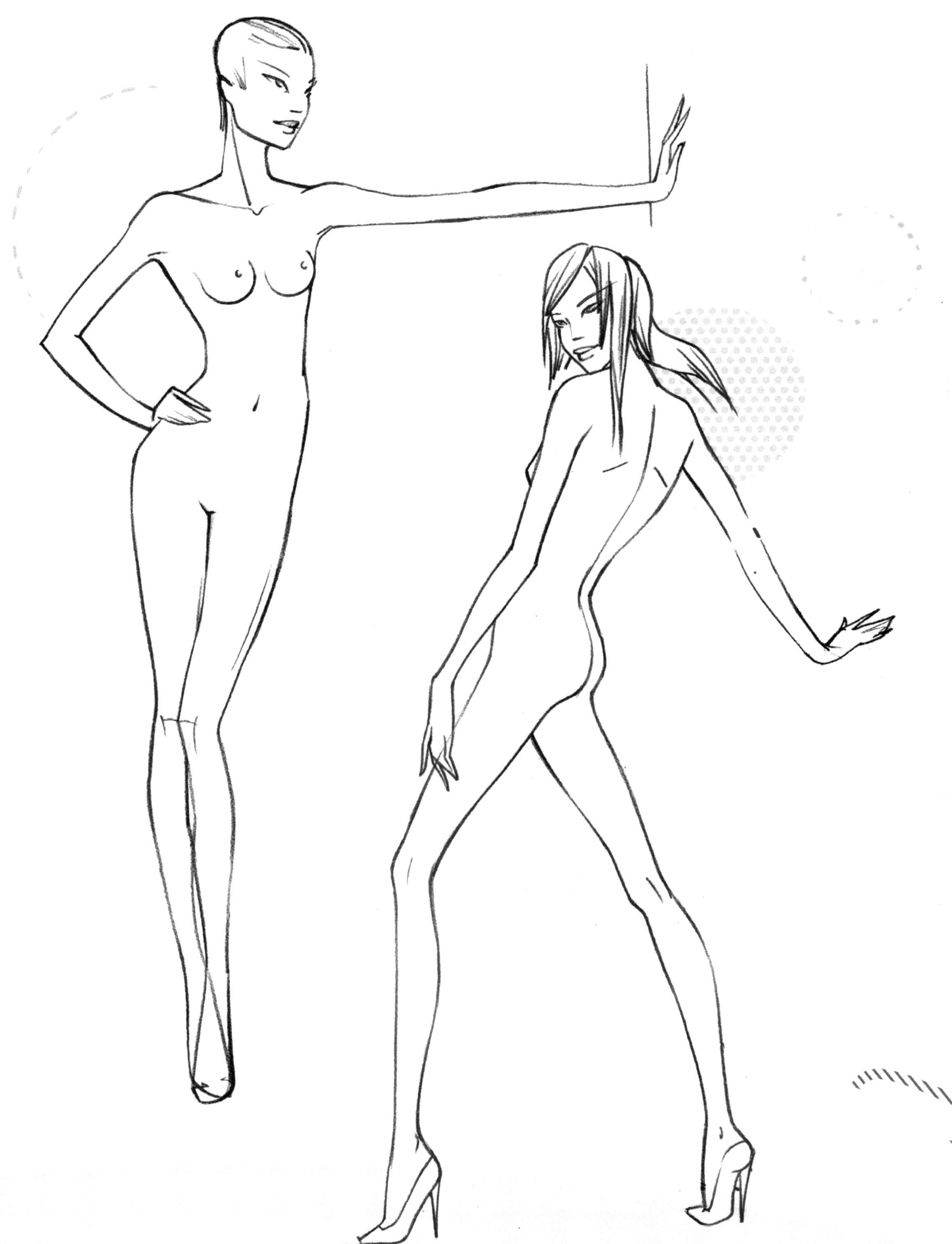

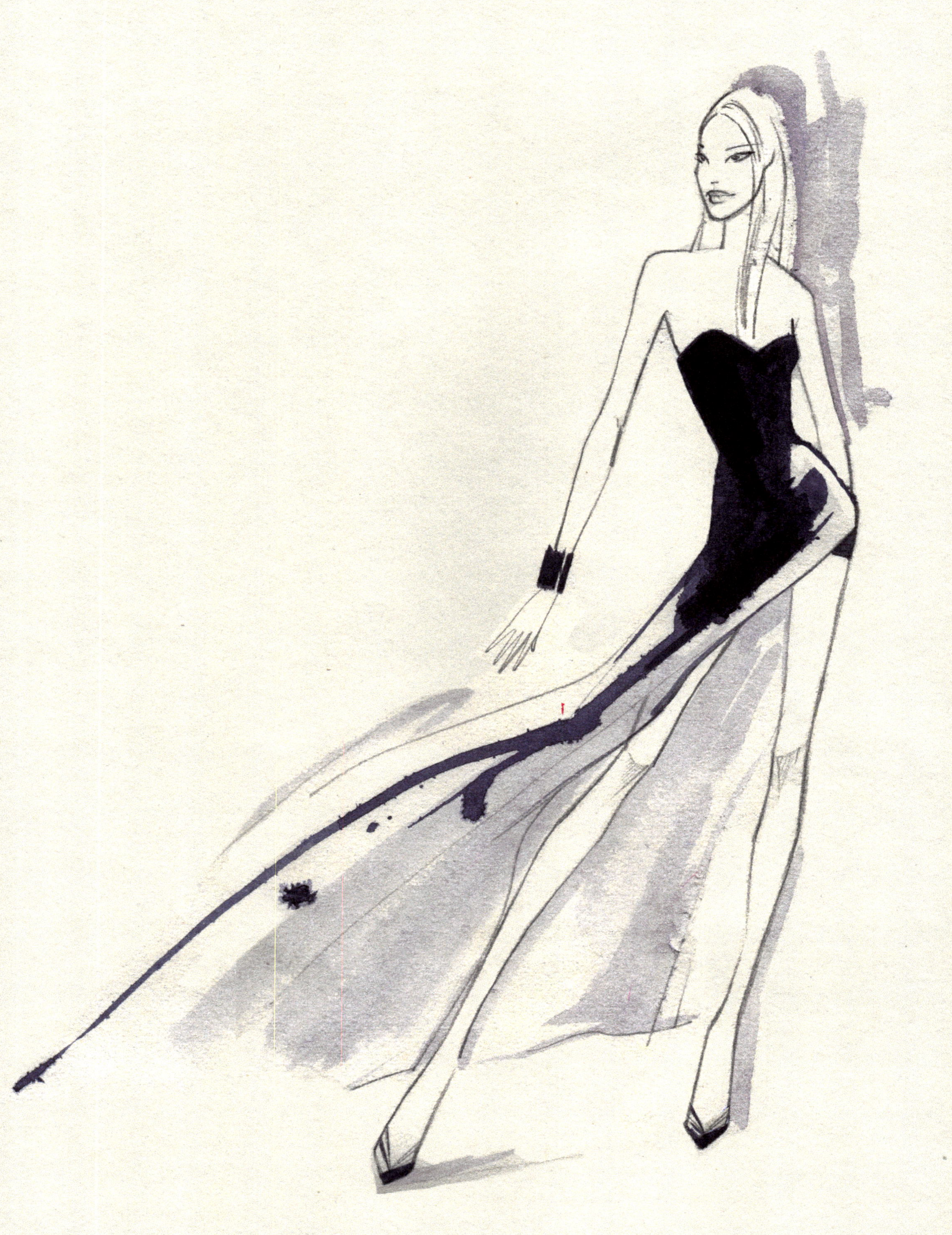

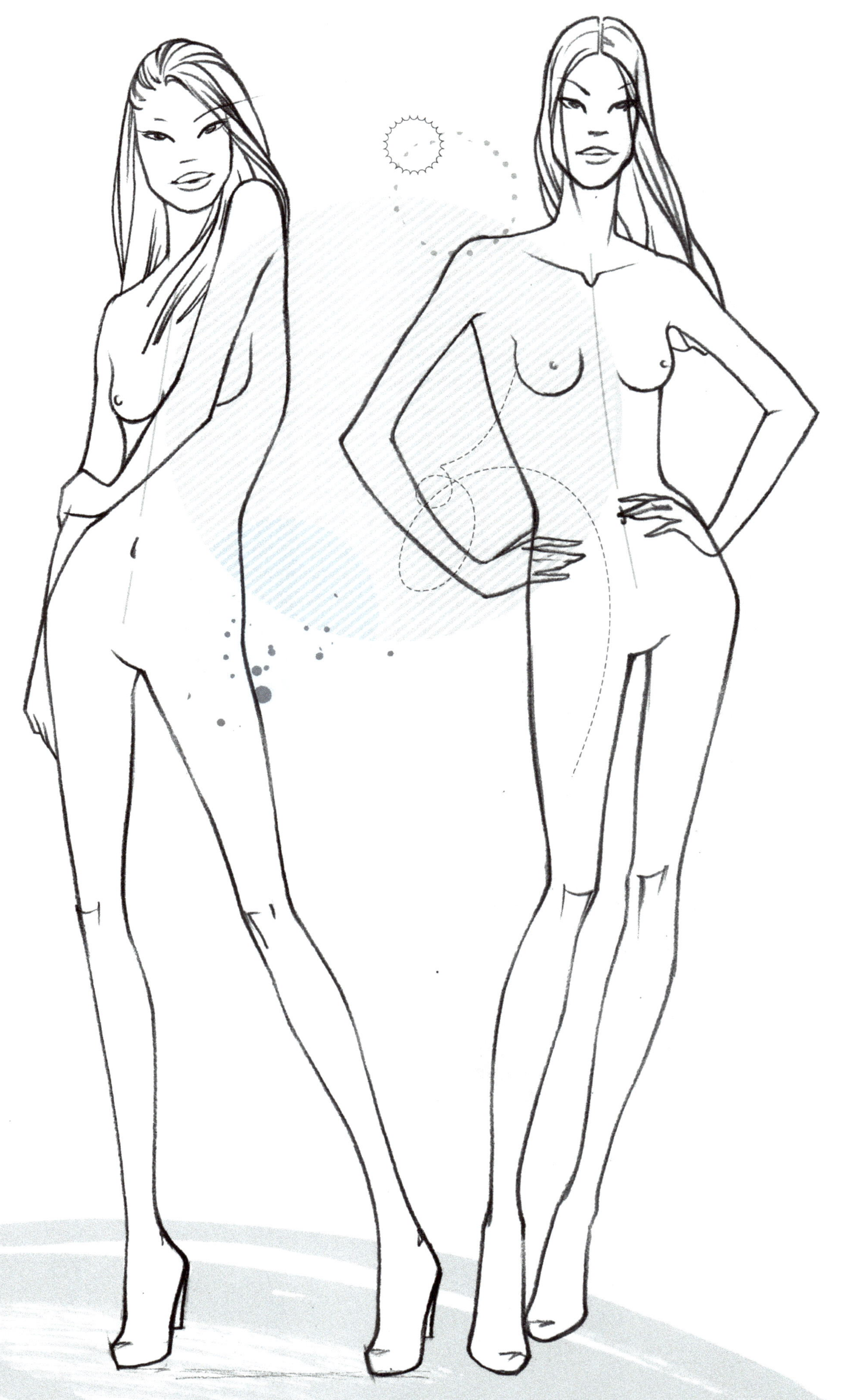

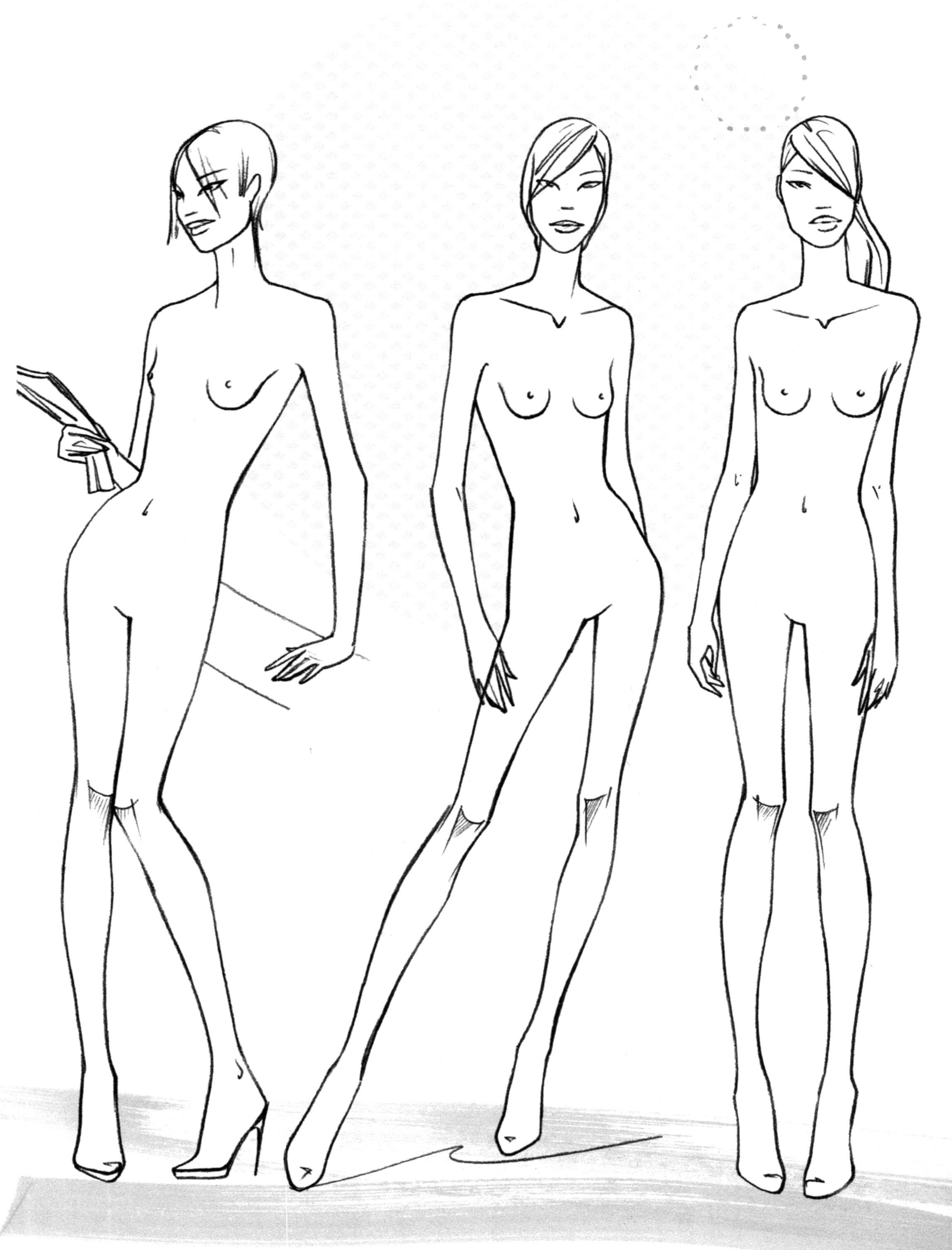

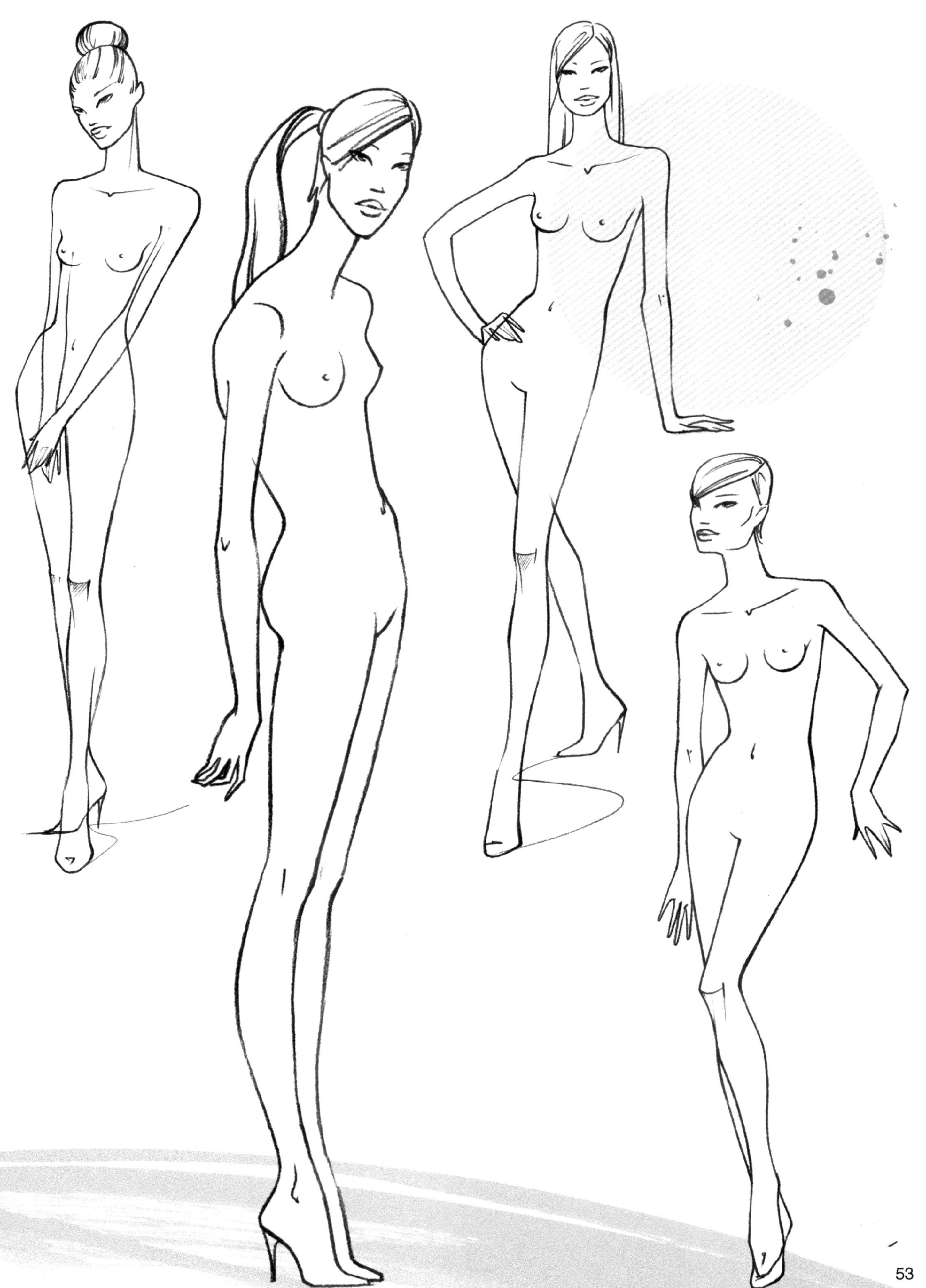

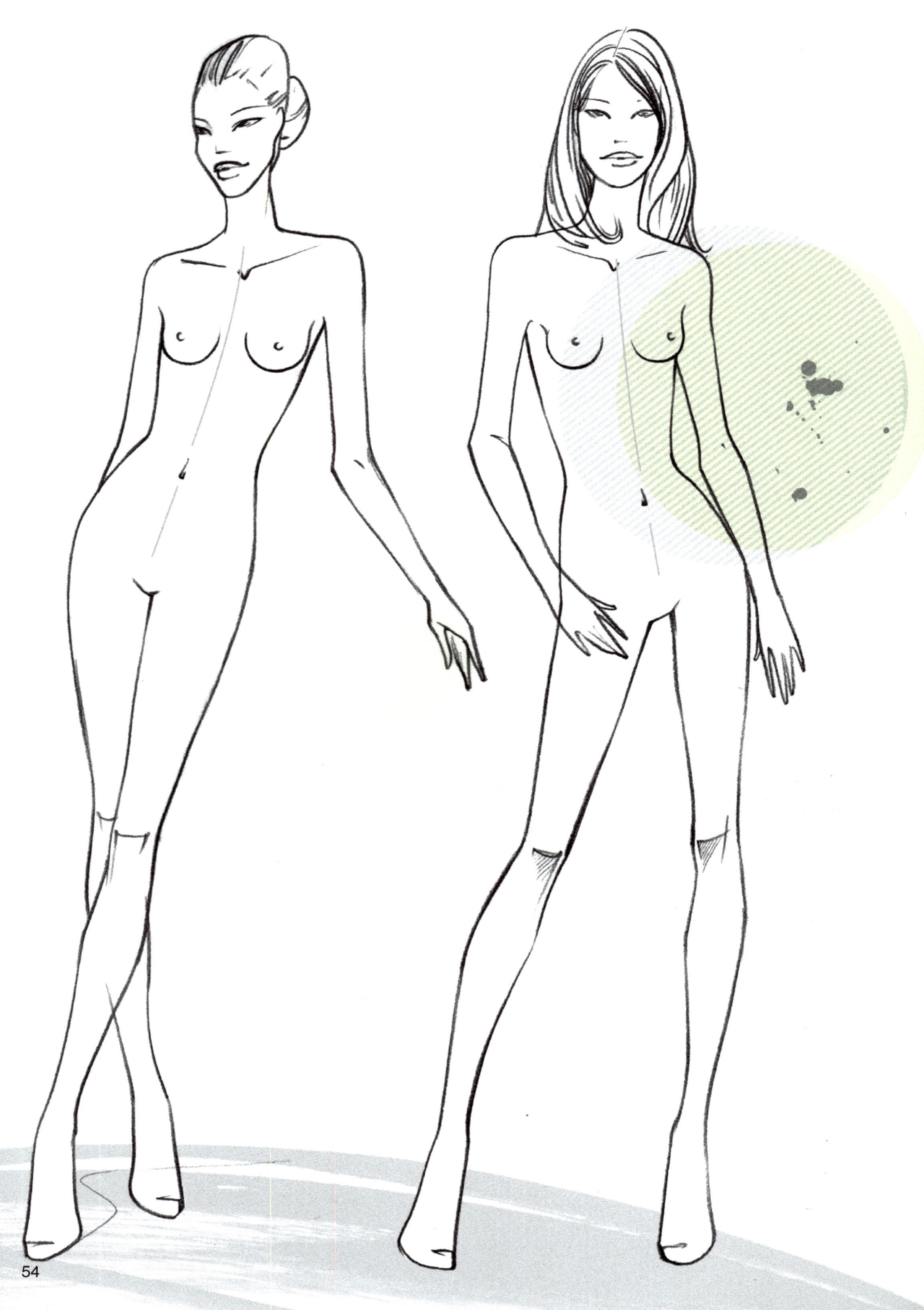

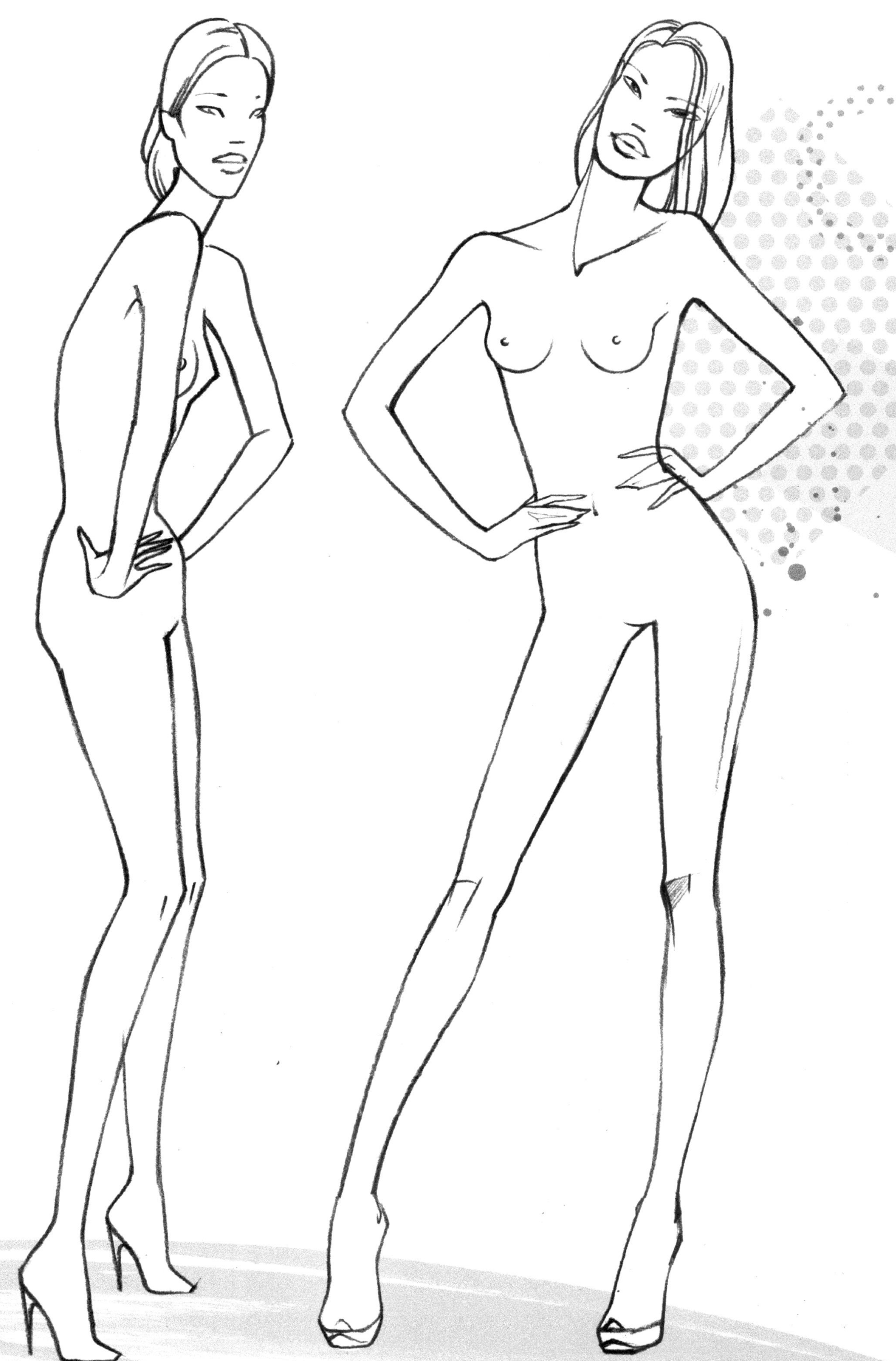

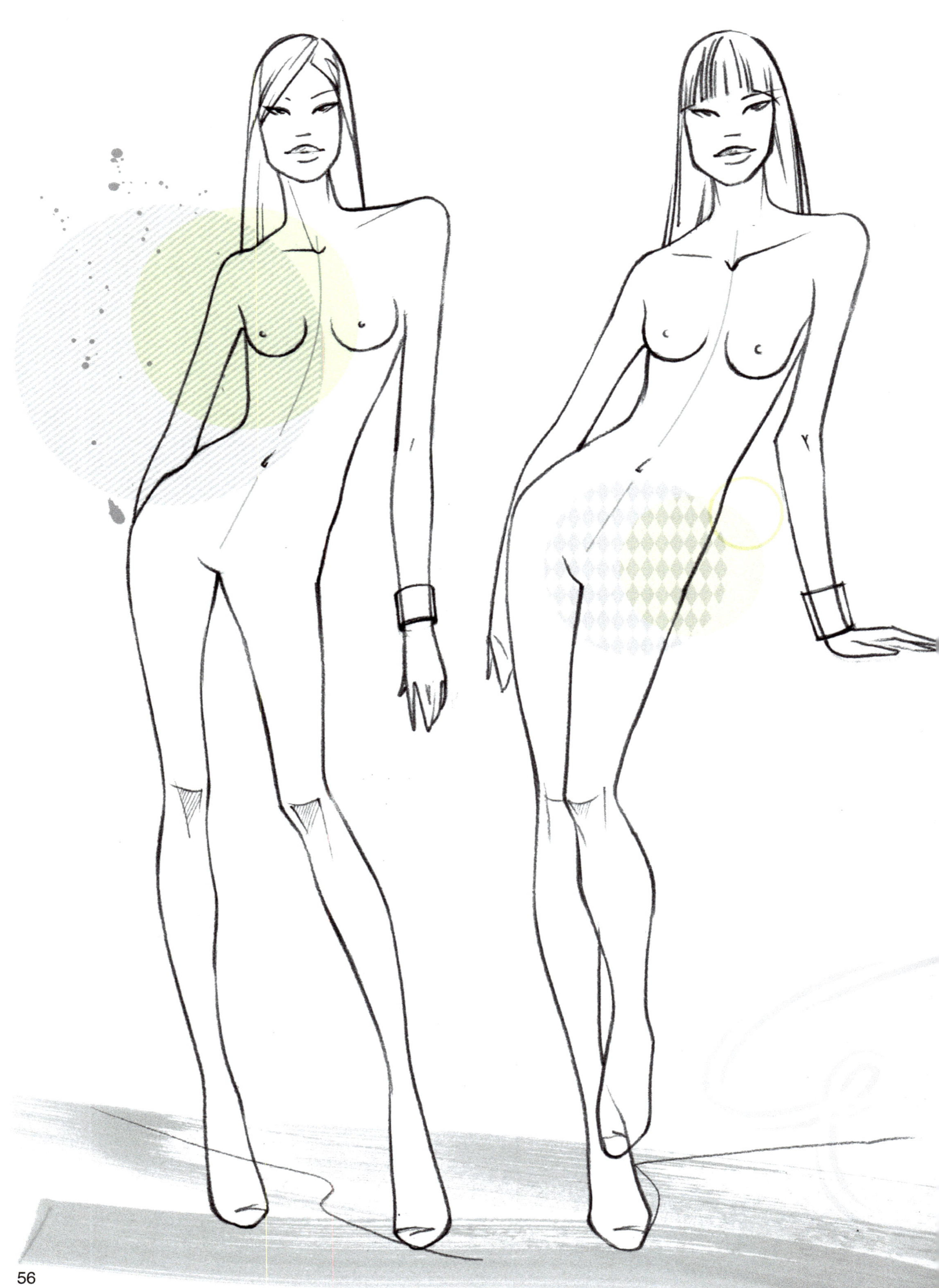

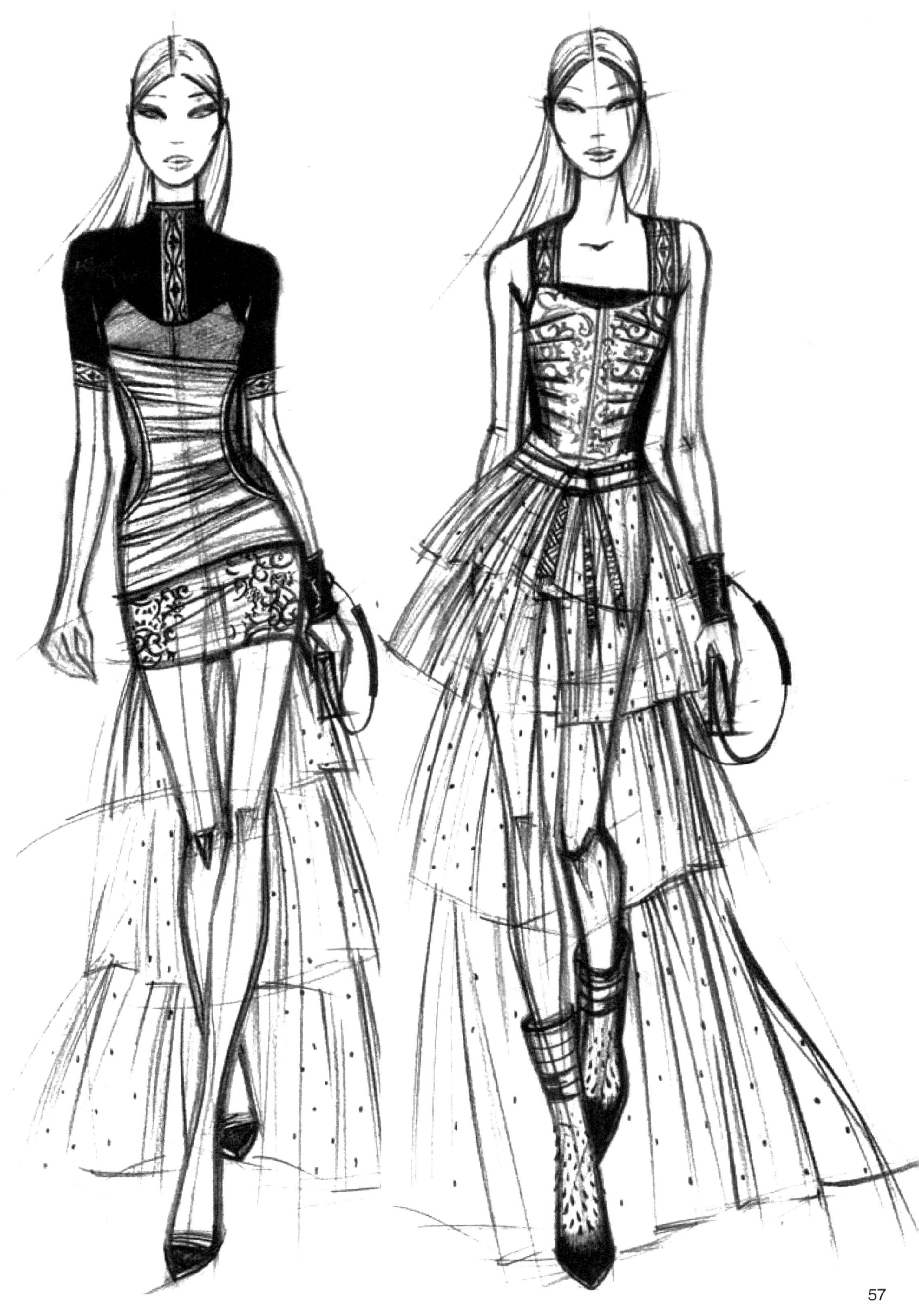

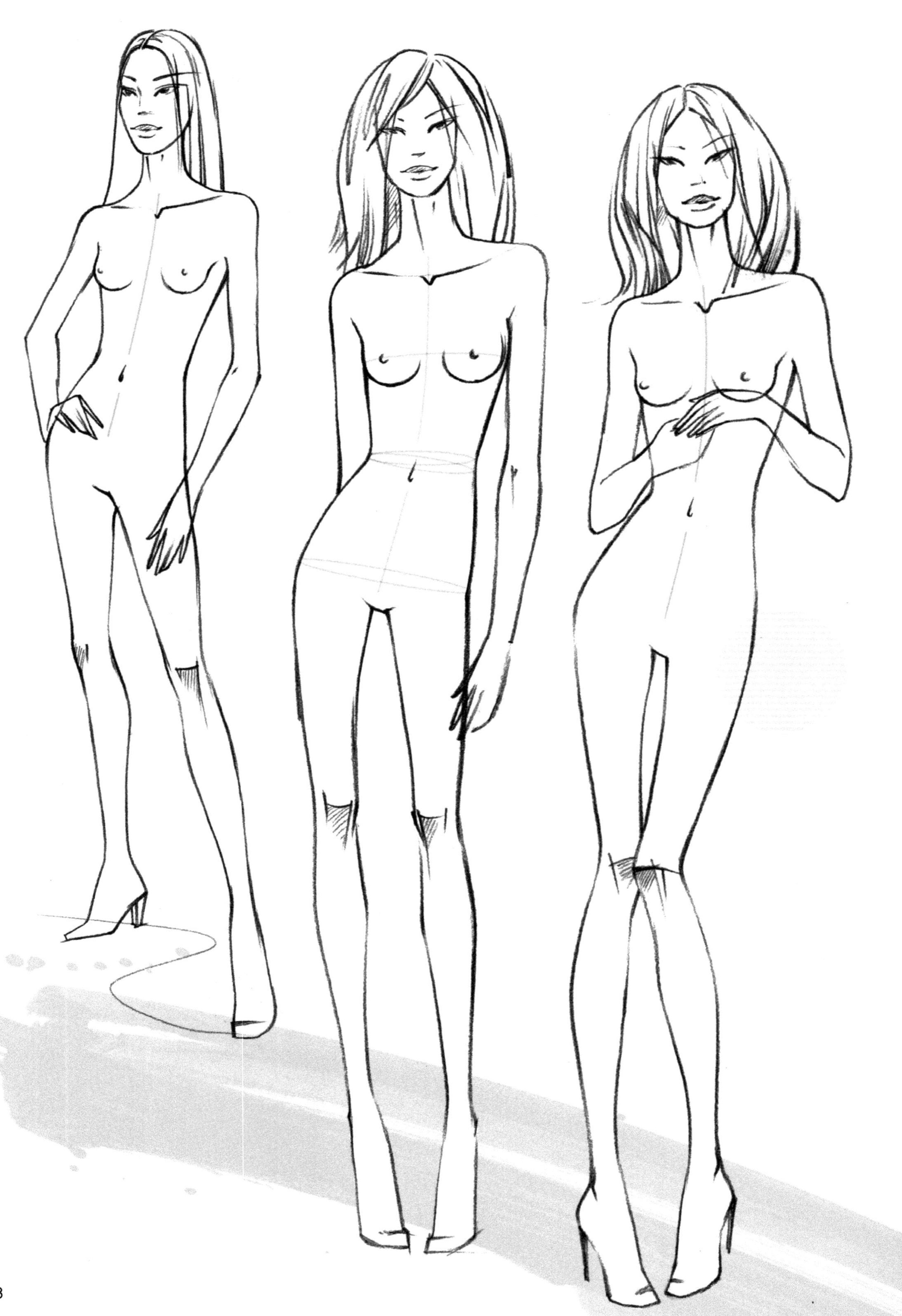

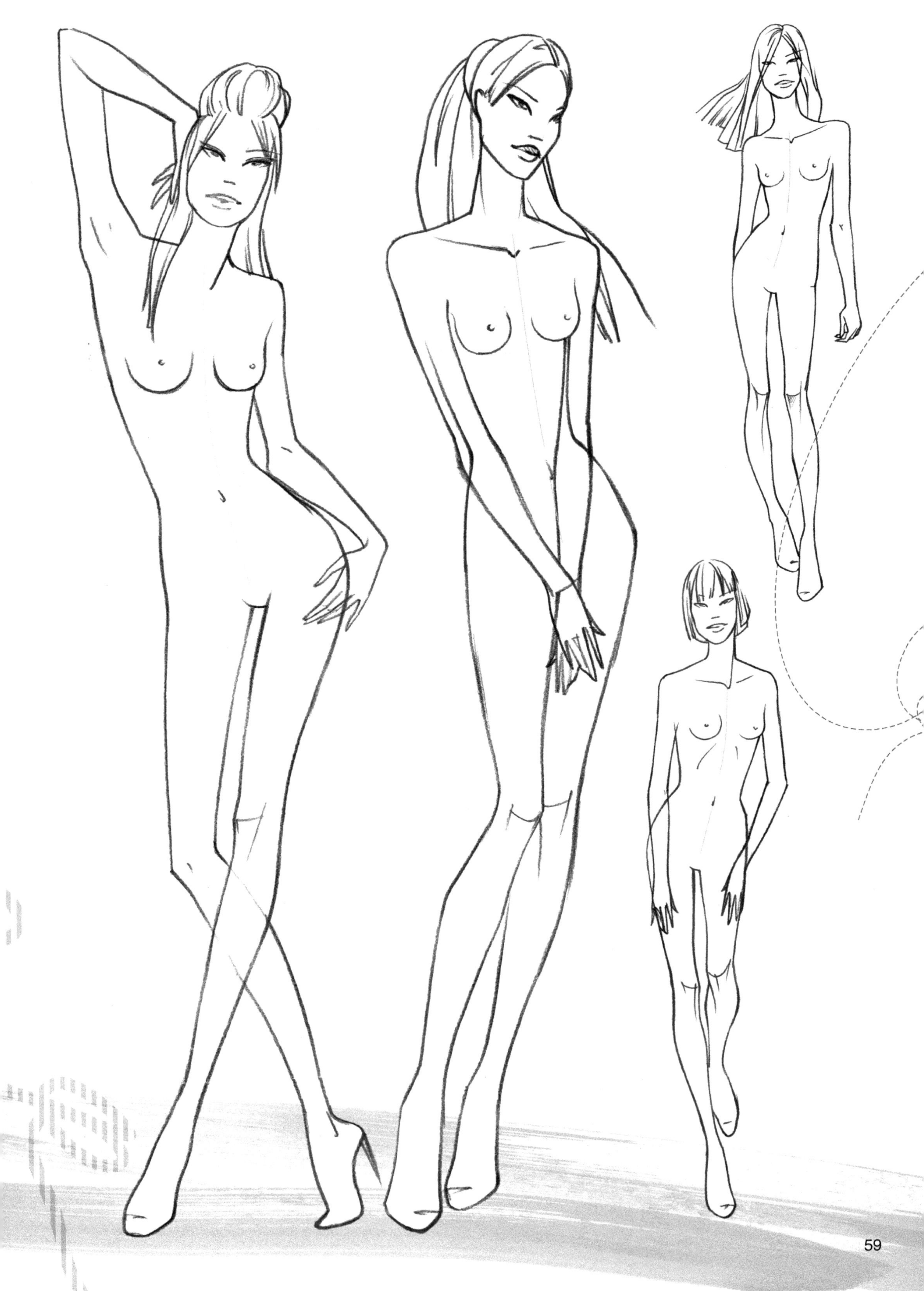

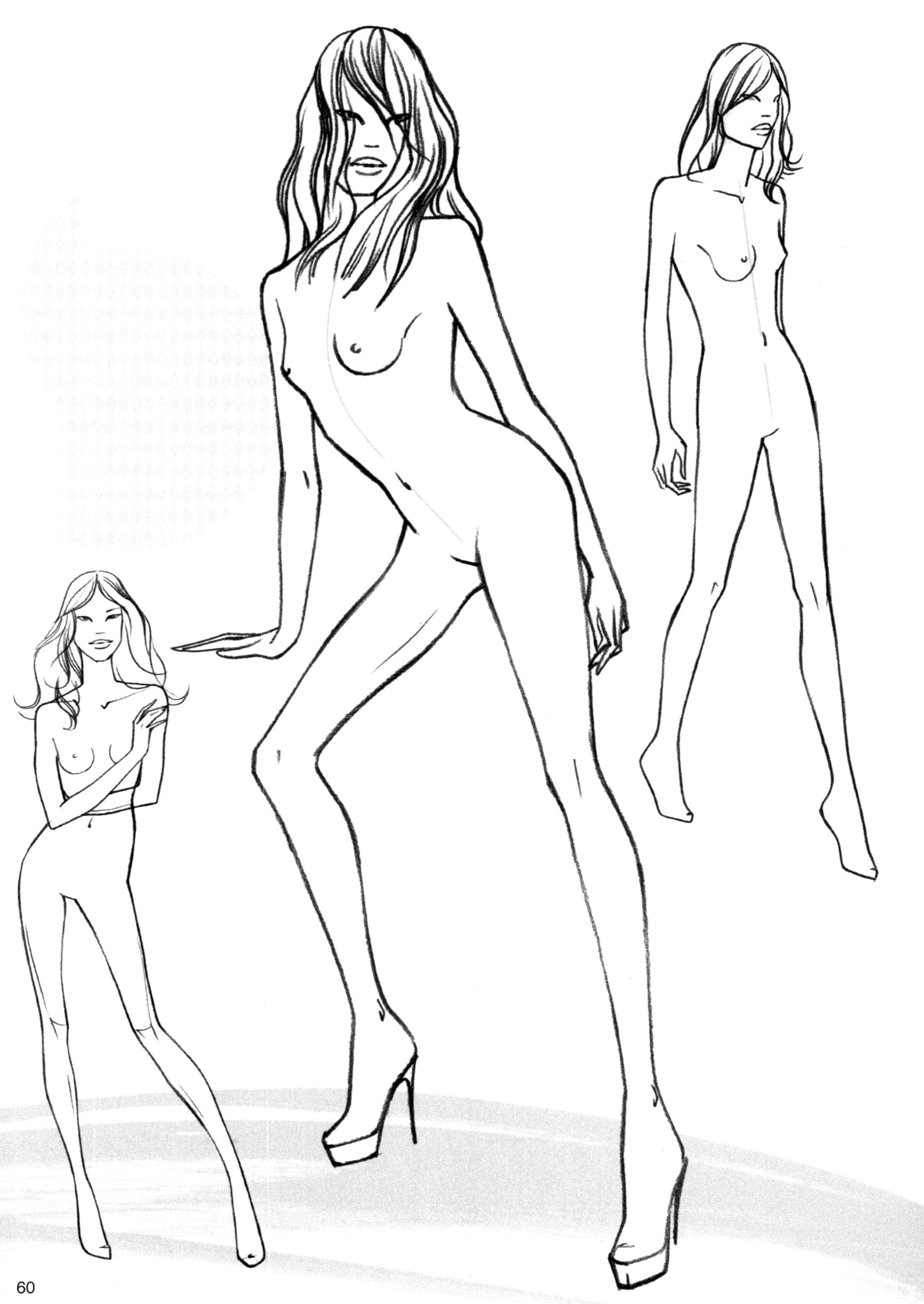

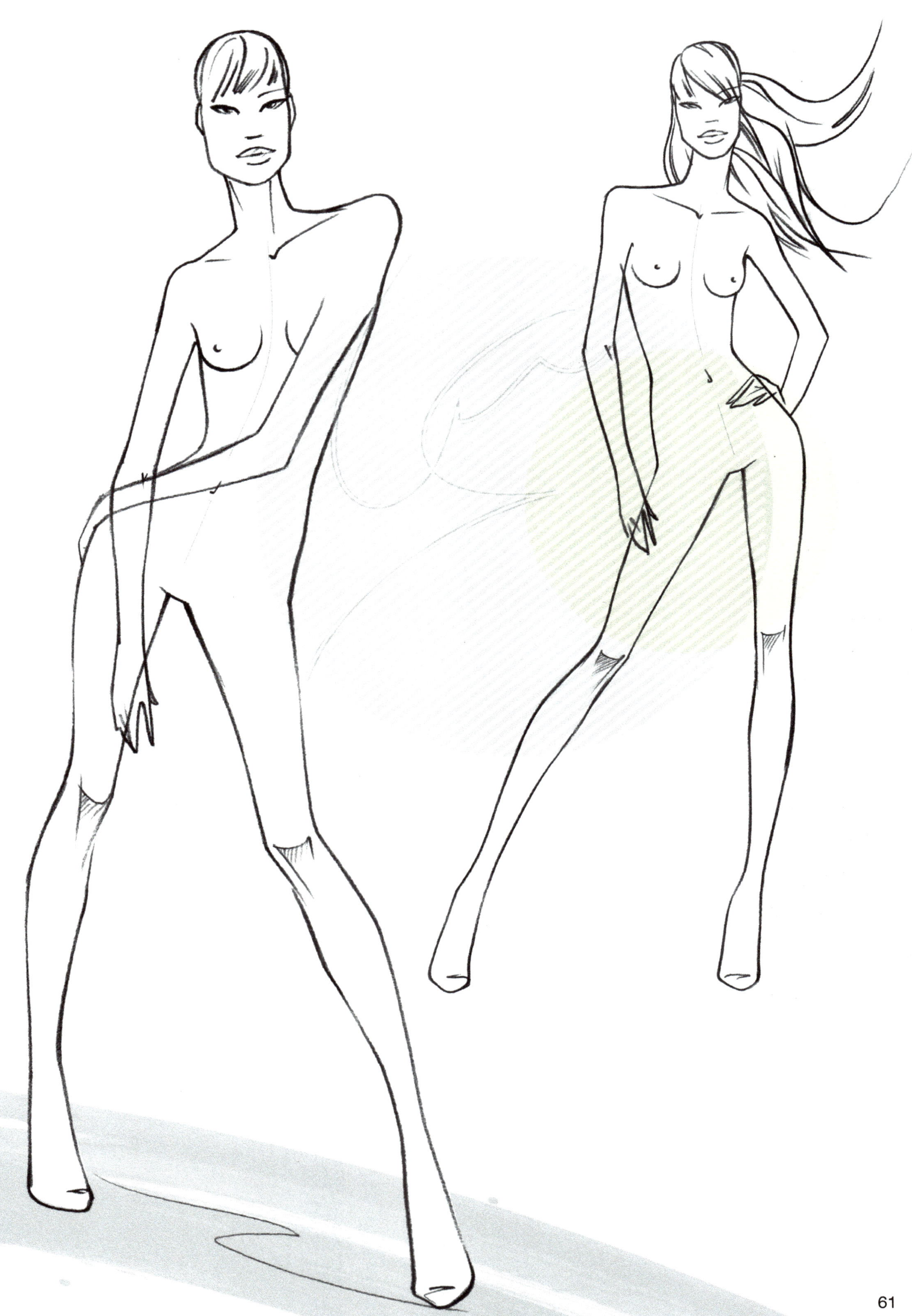

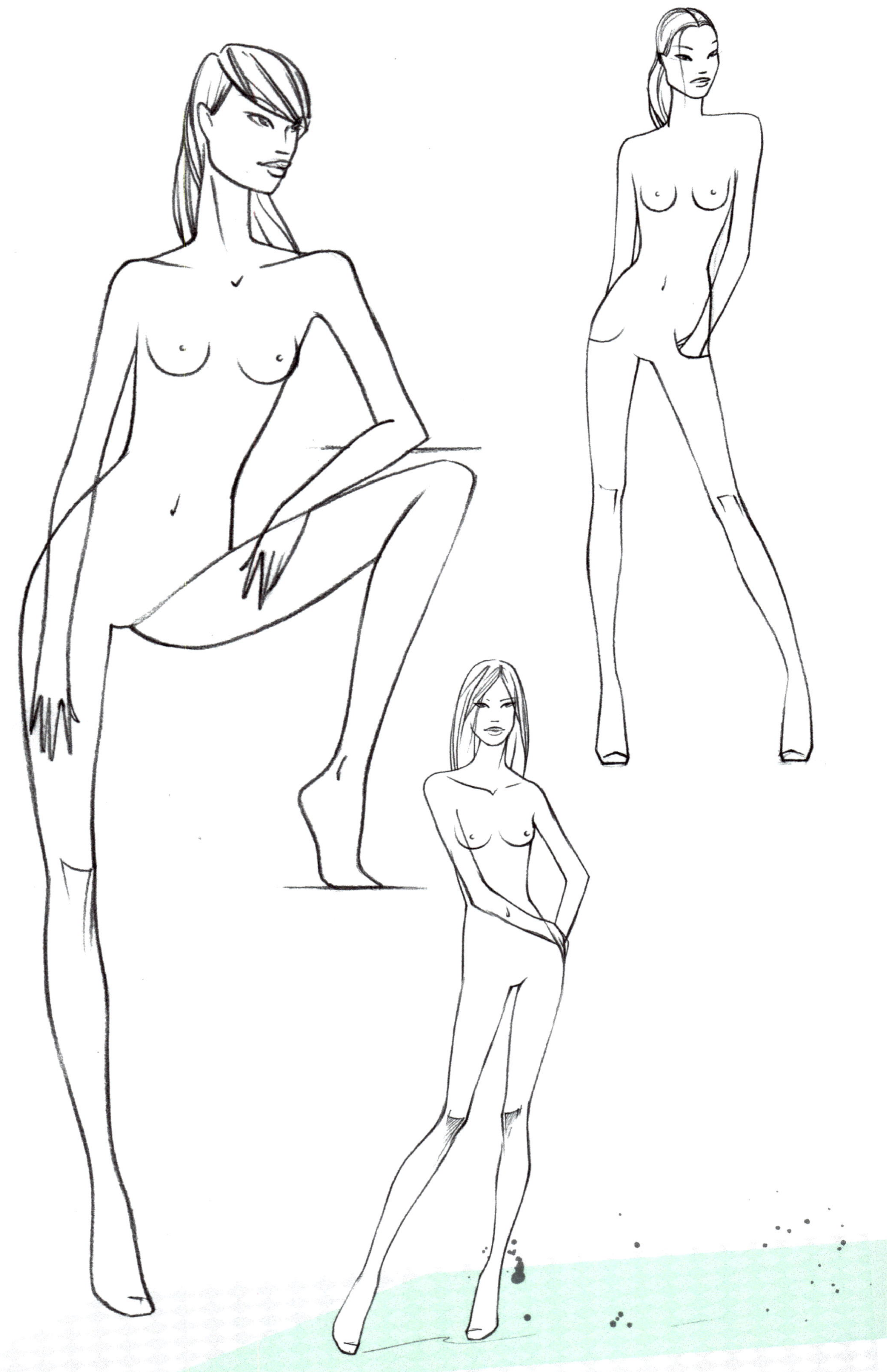

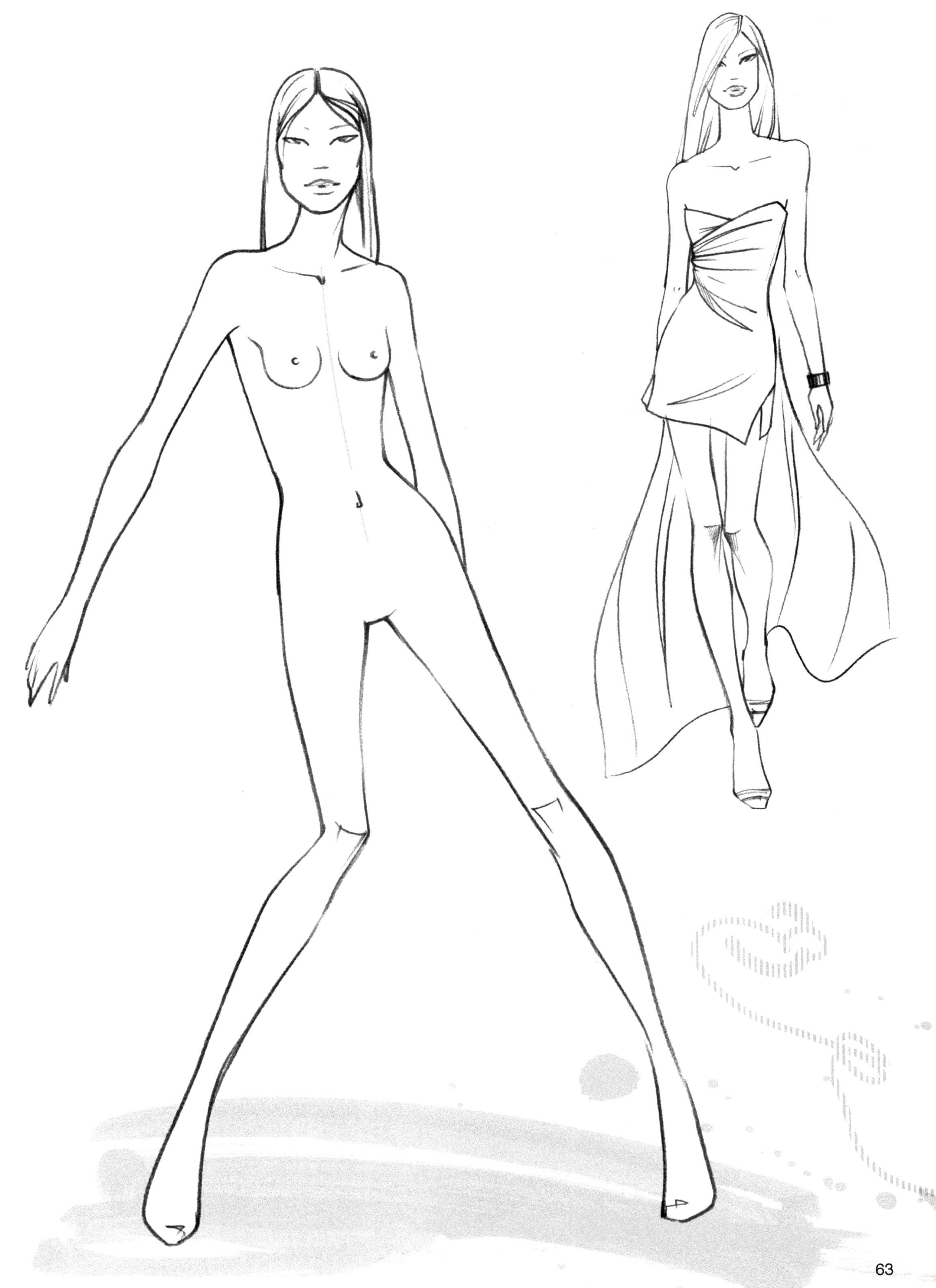

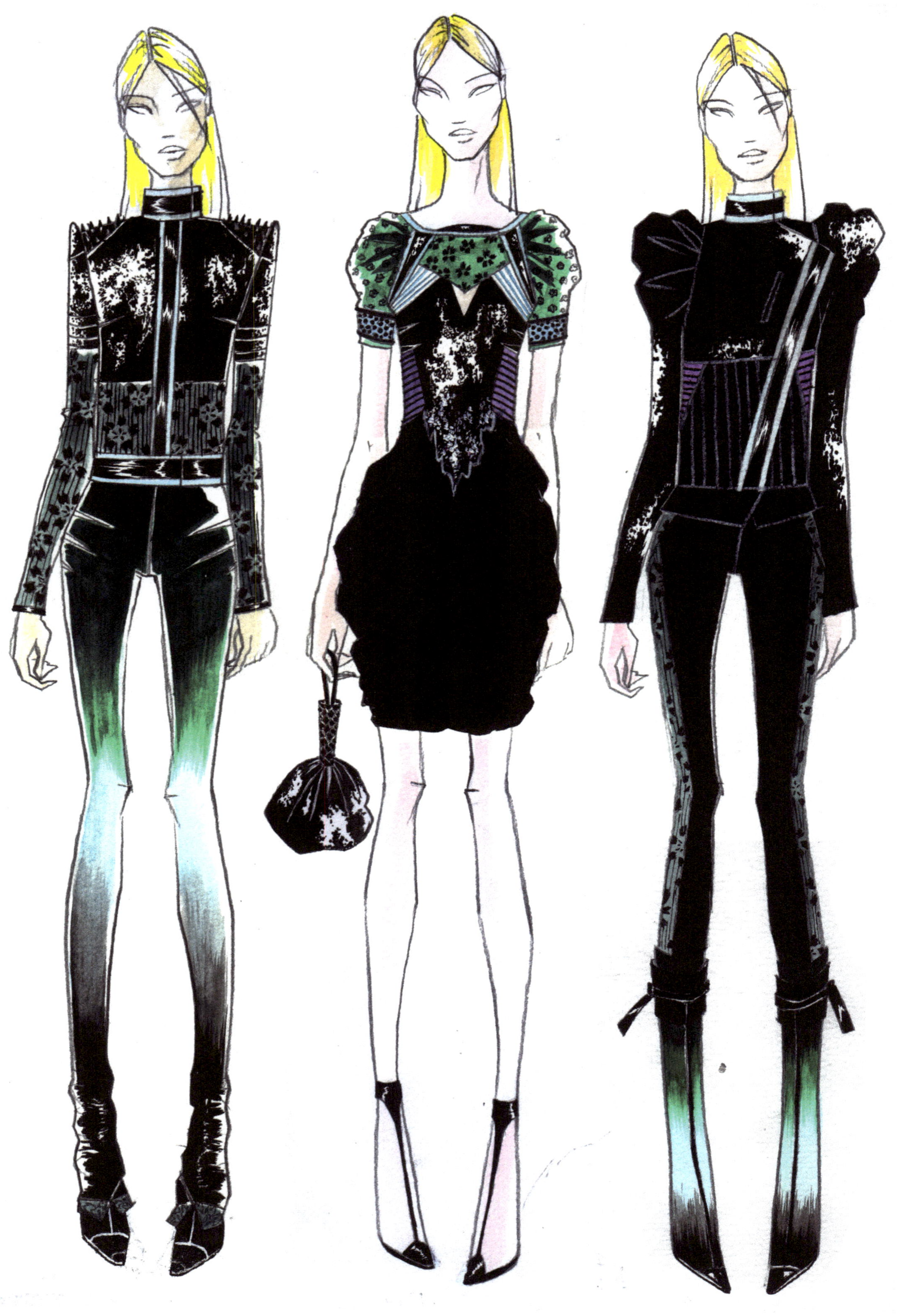

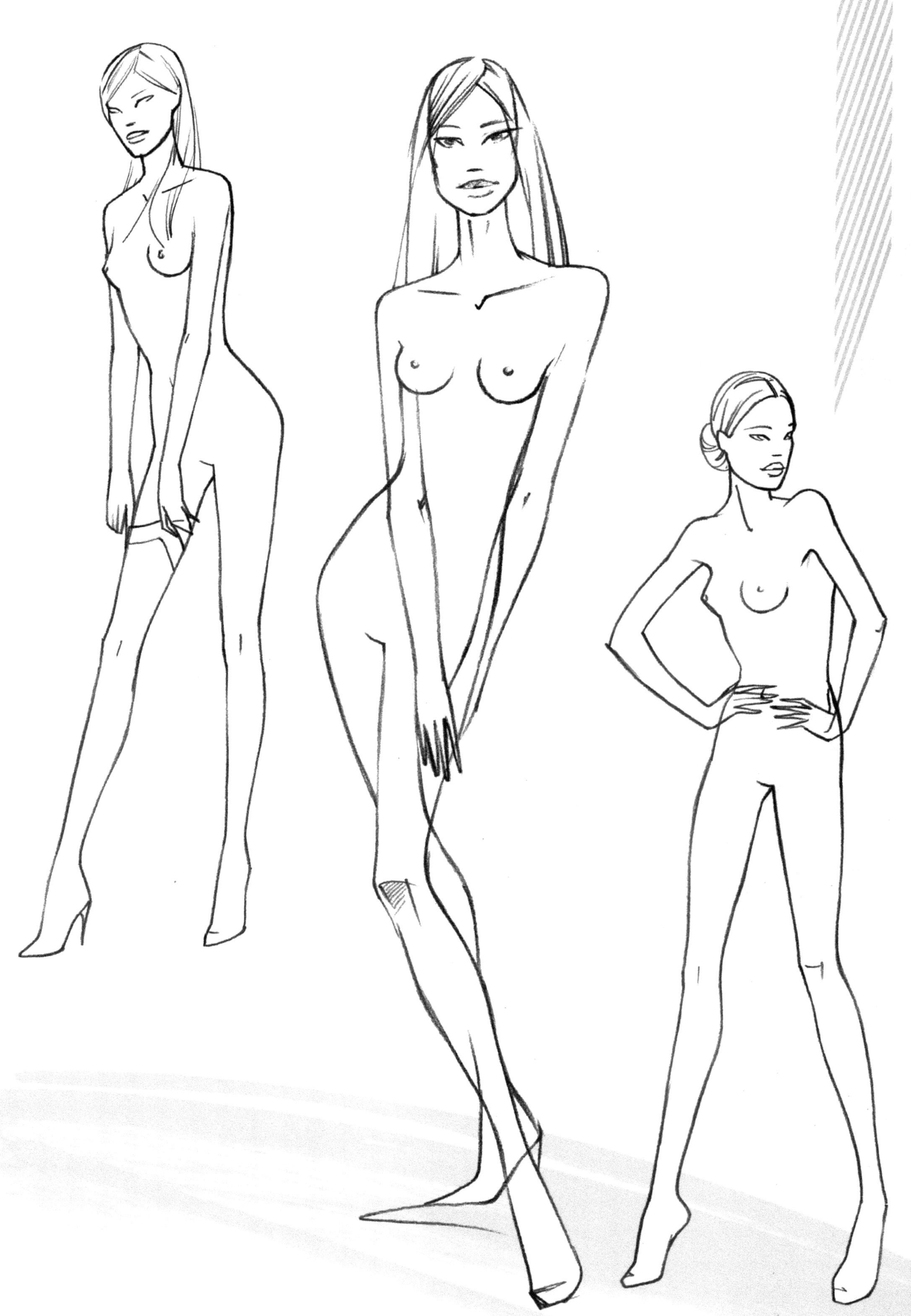

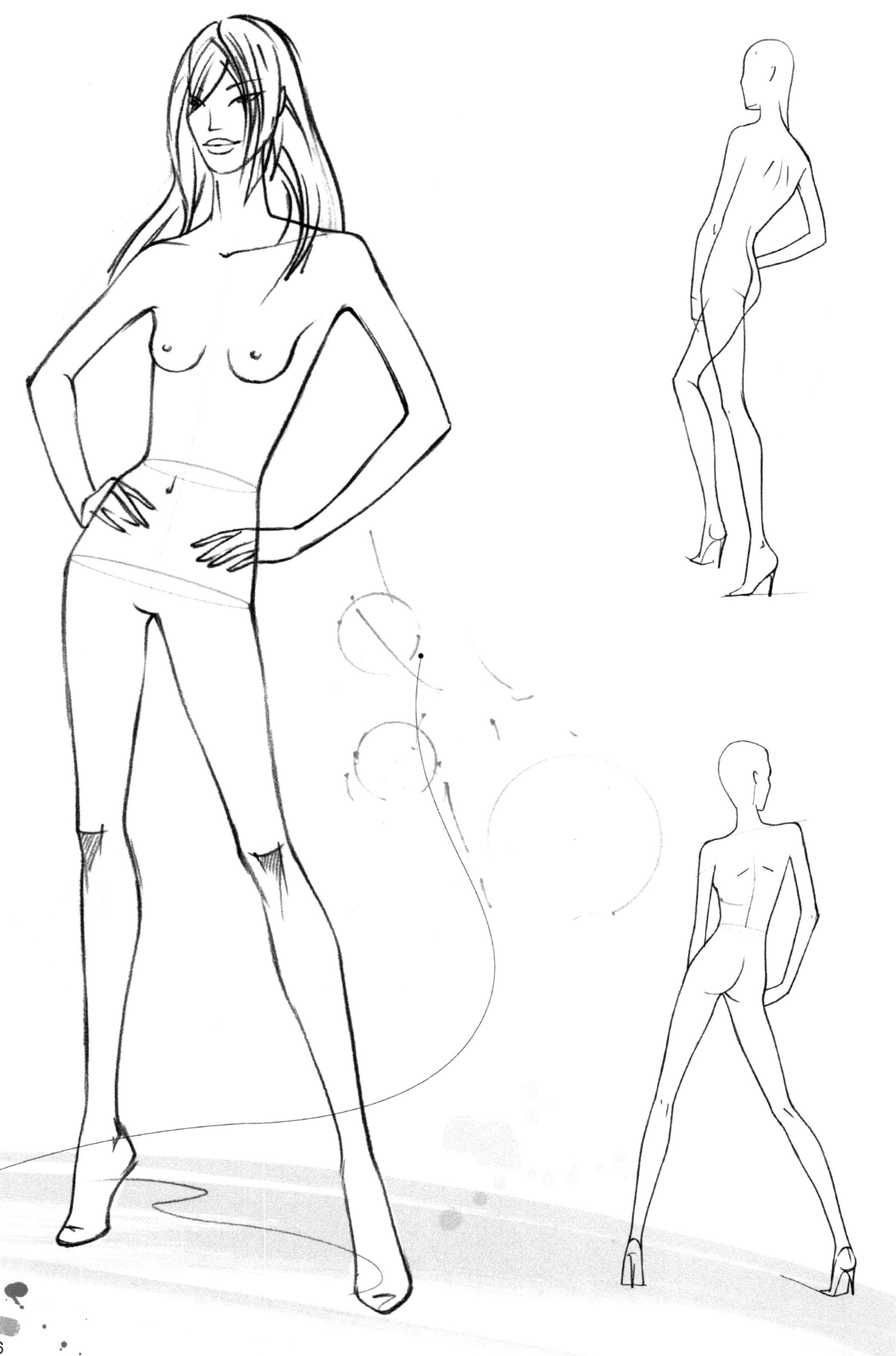

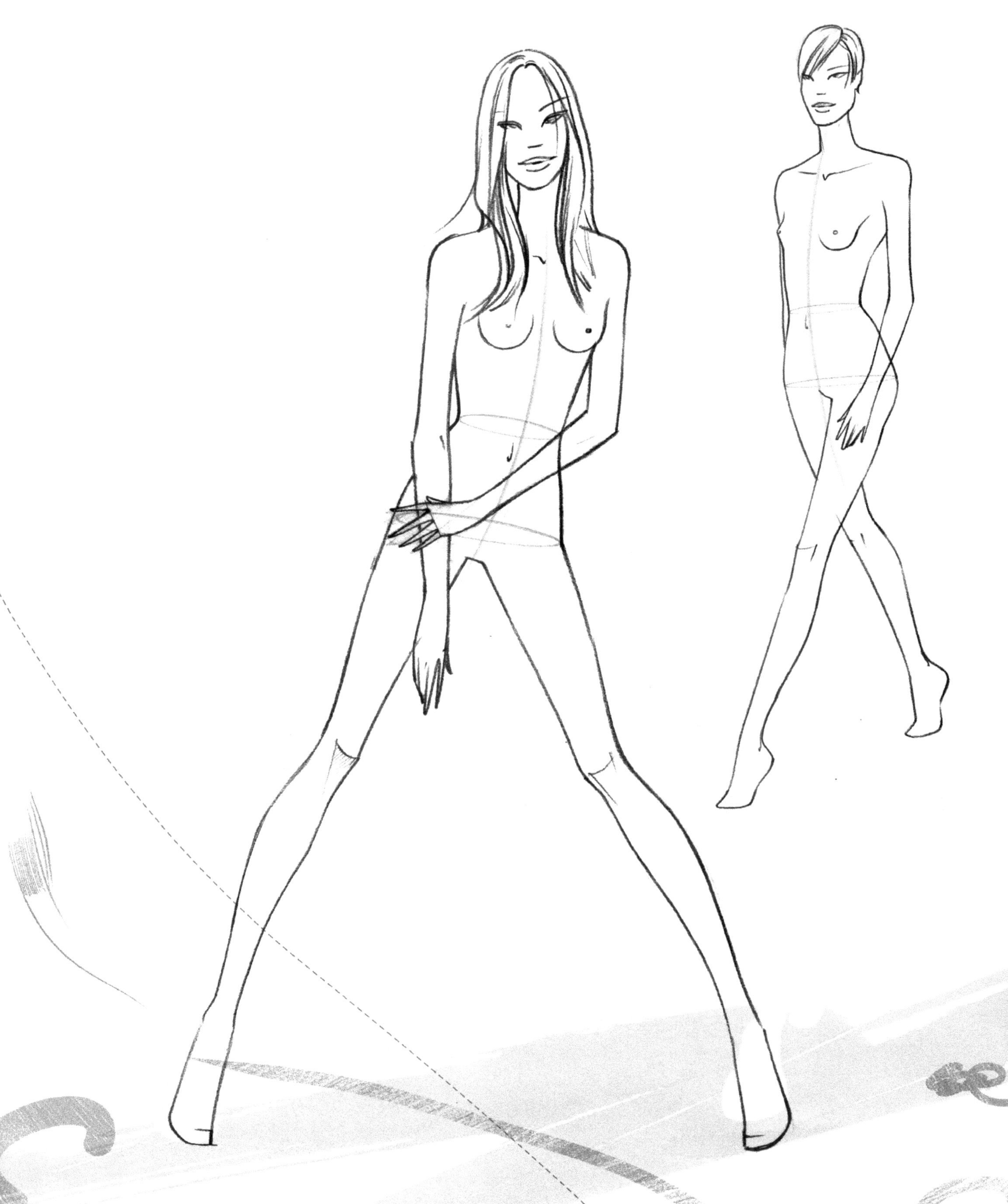

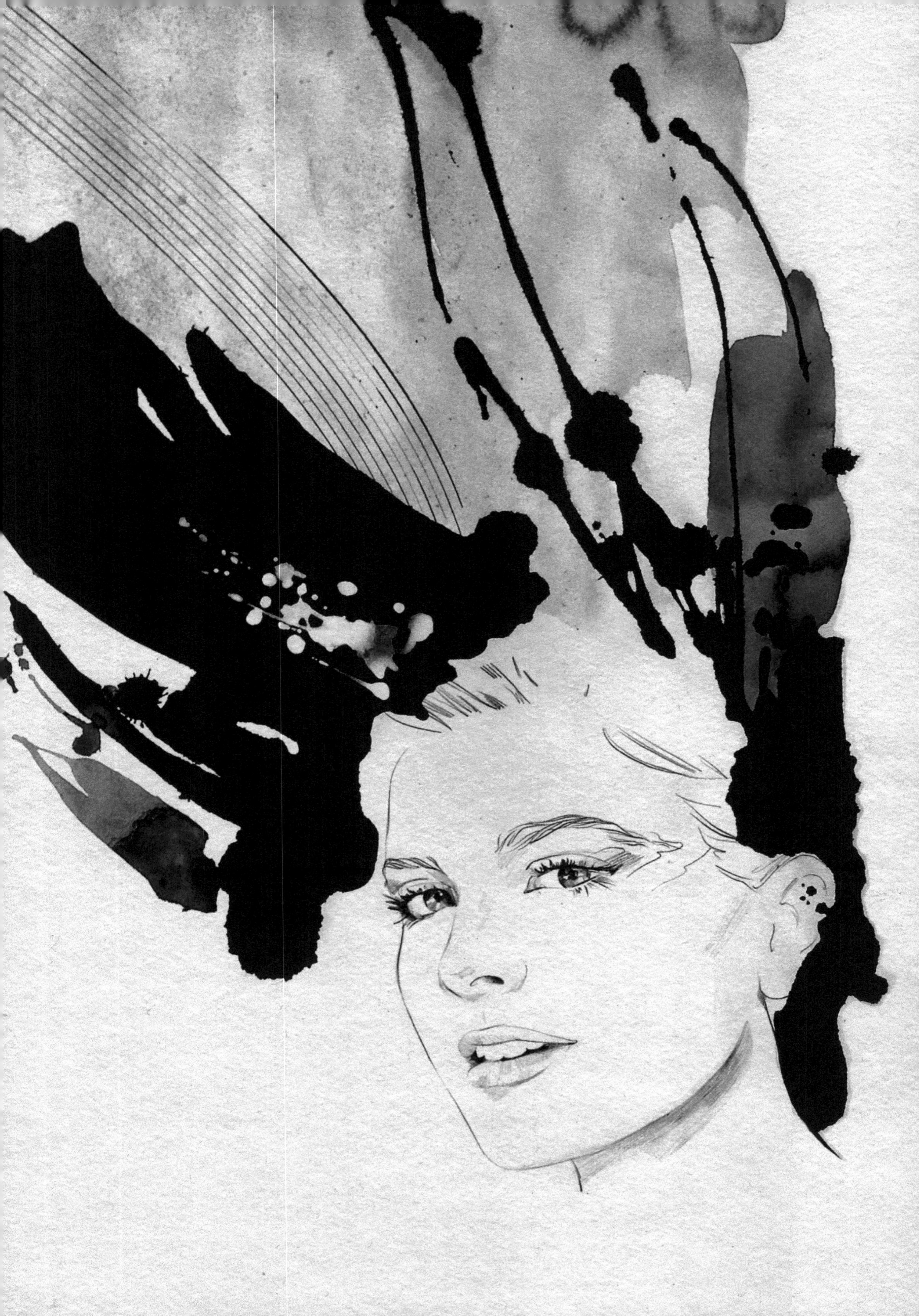

FACES

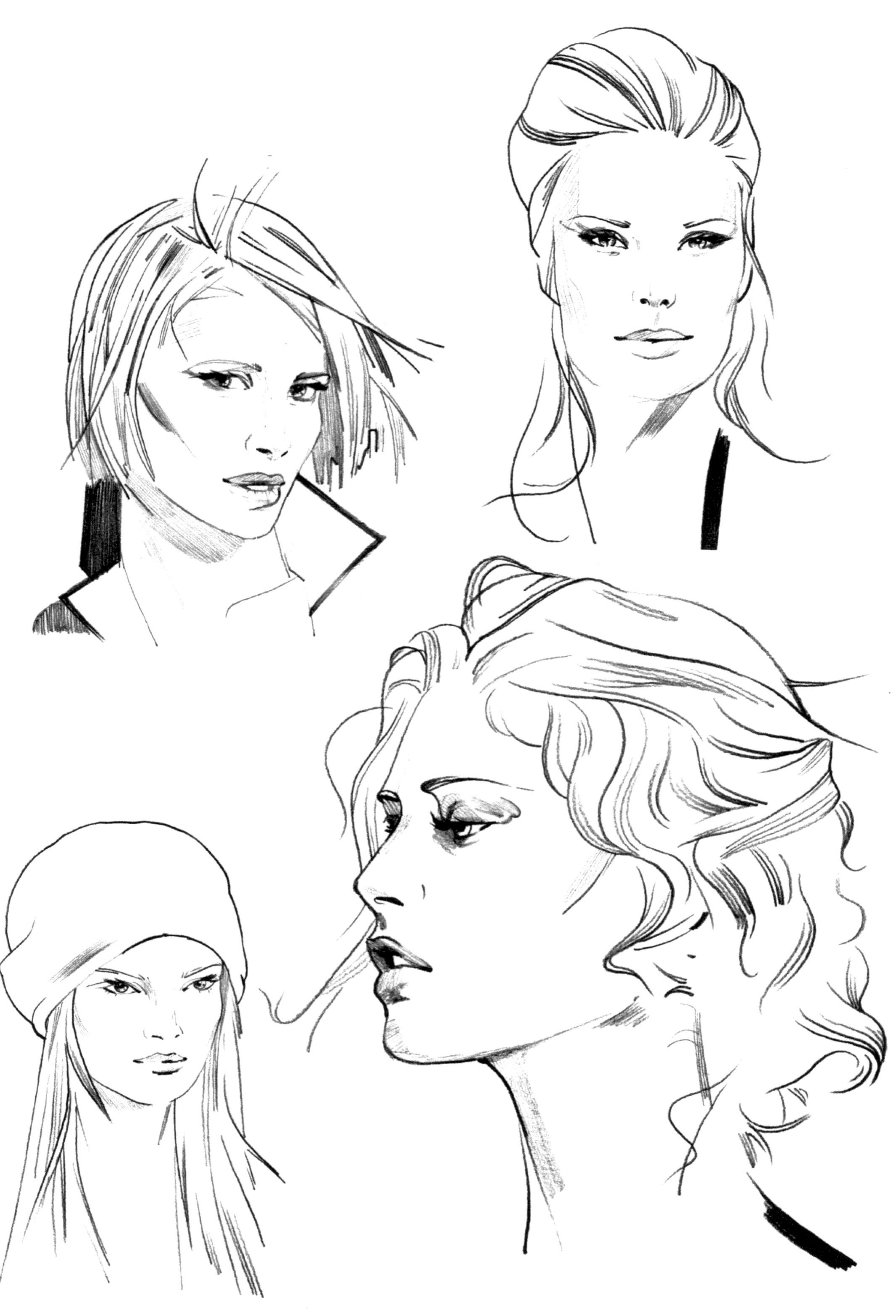

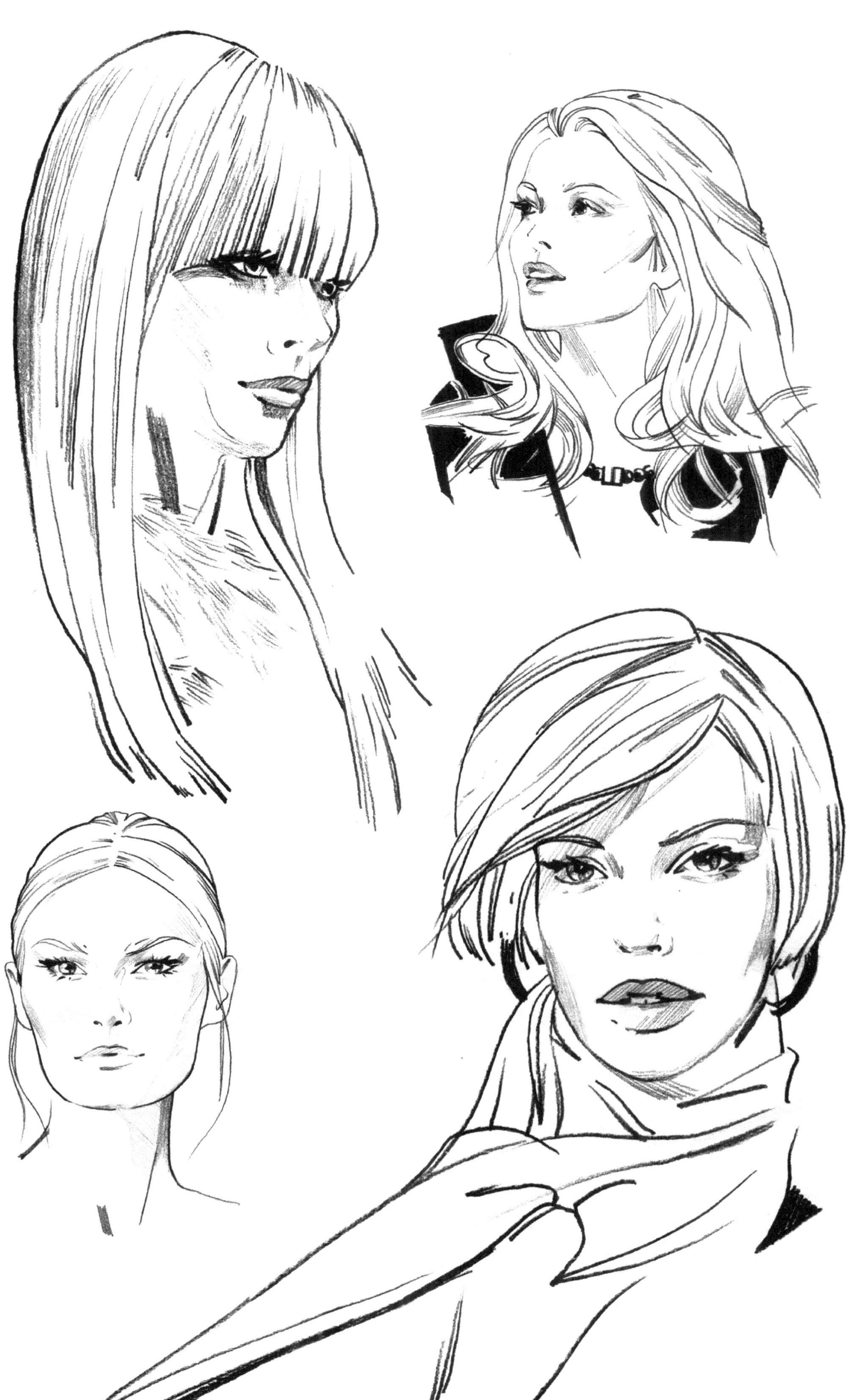

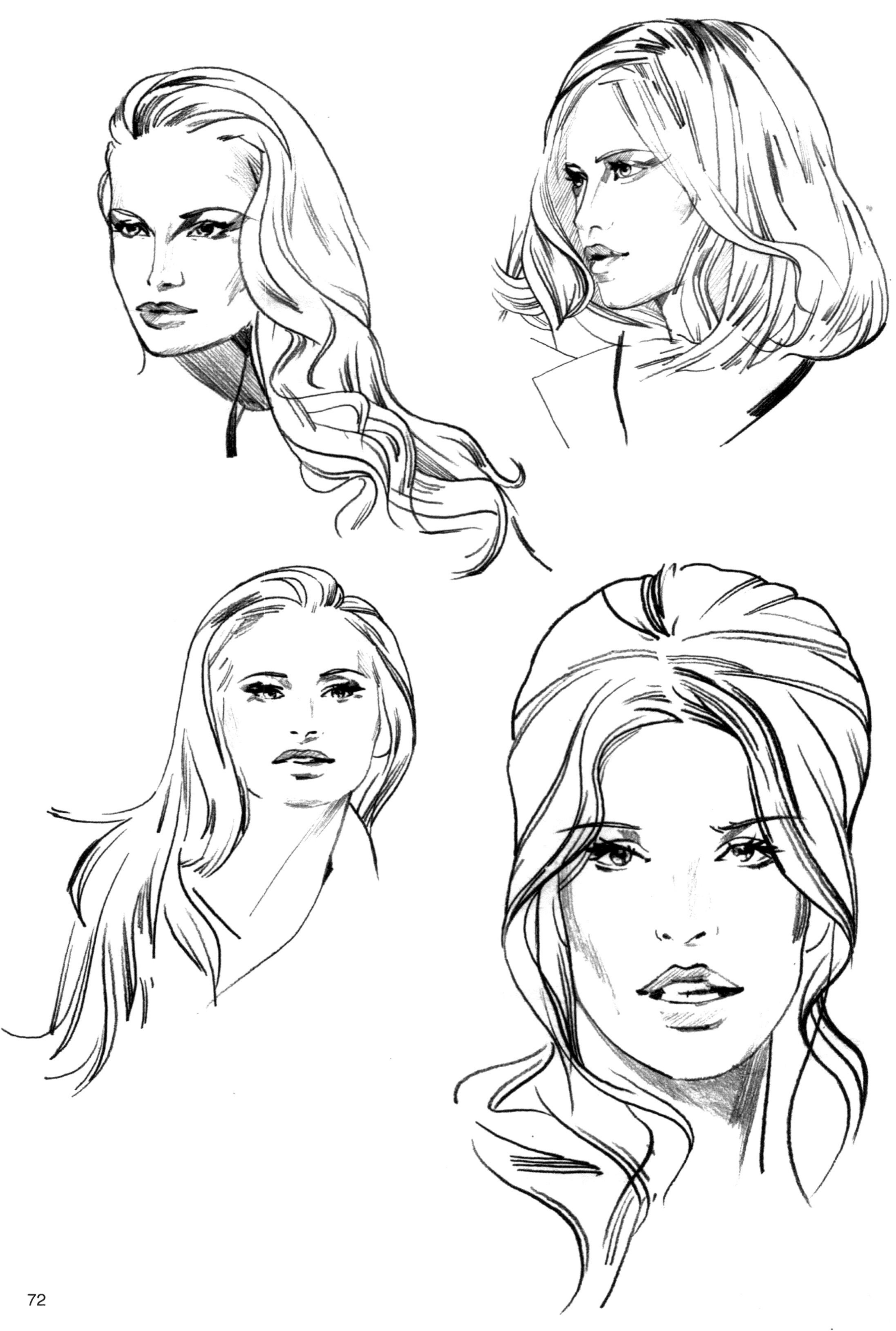

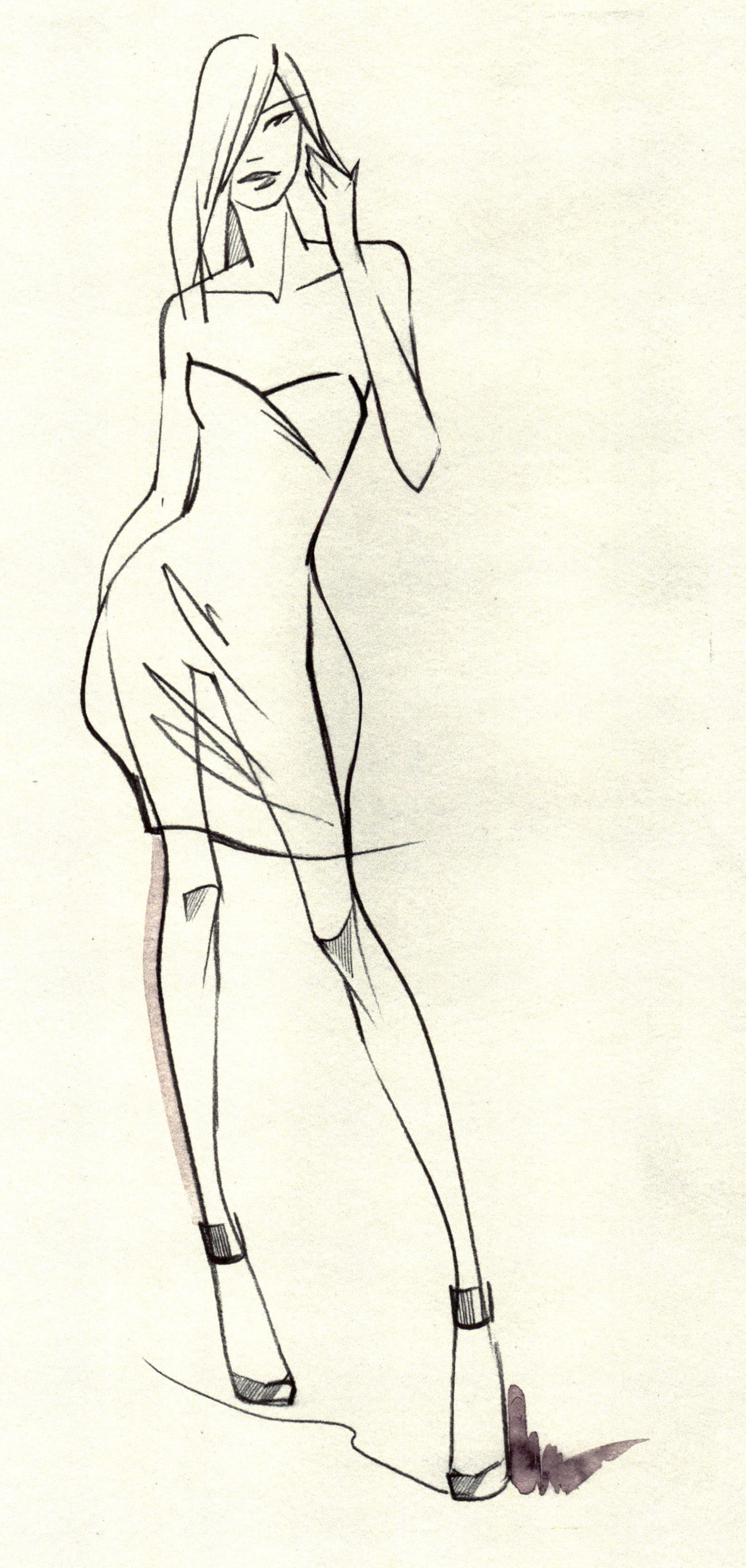

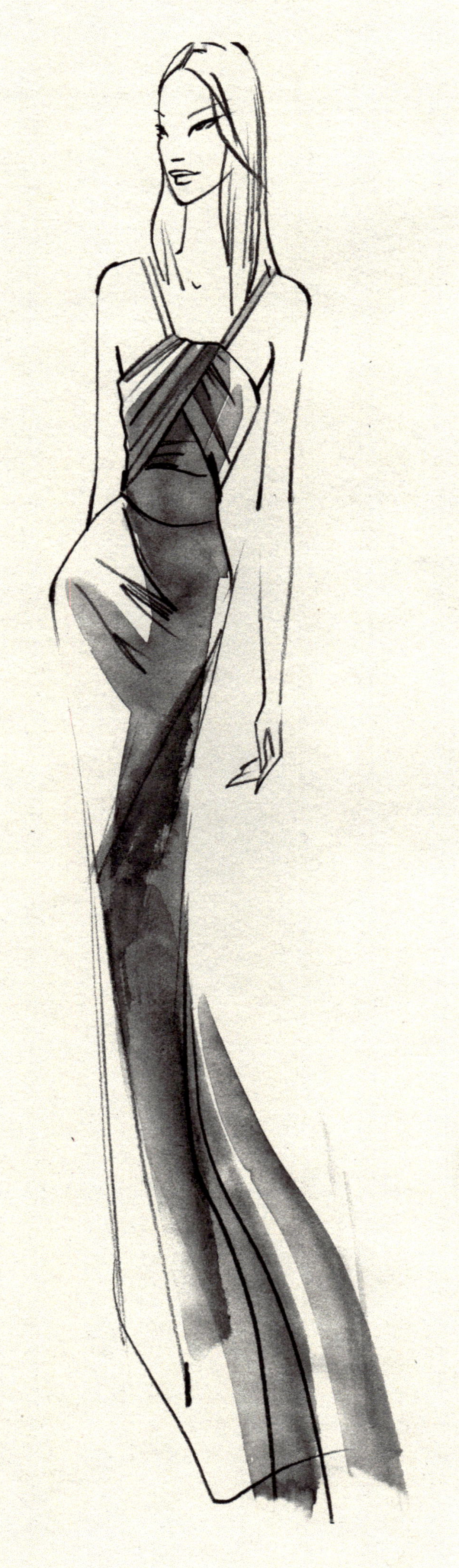

HANDS

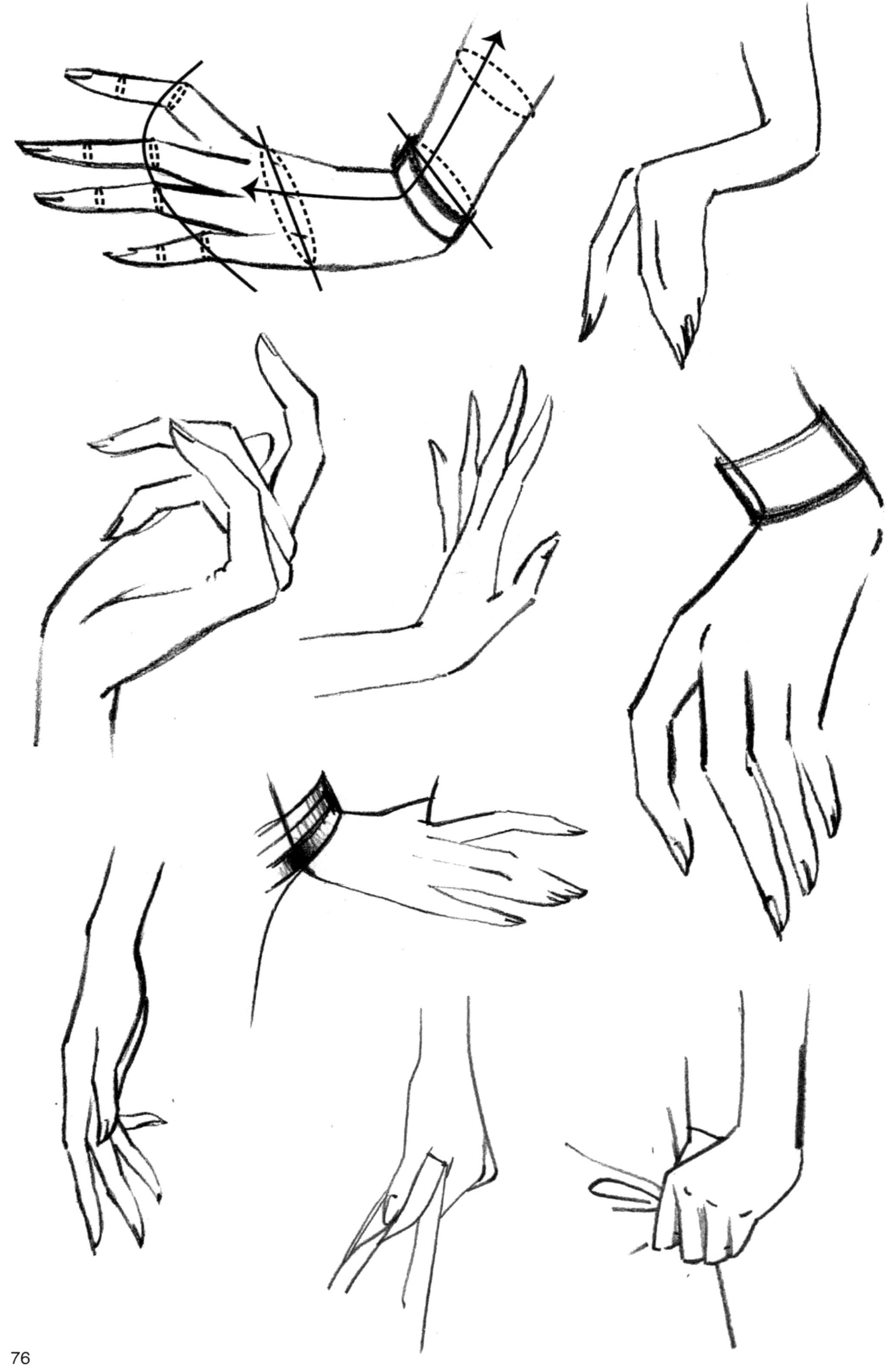

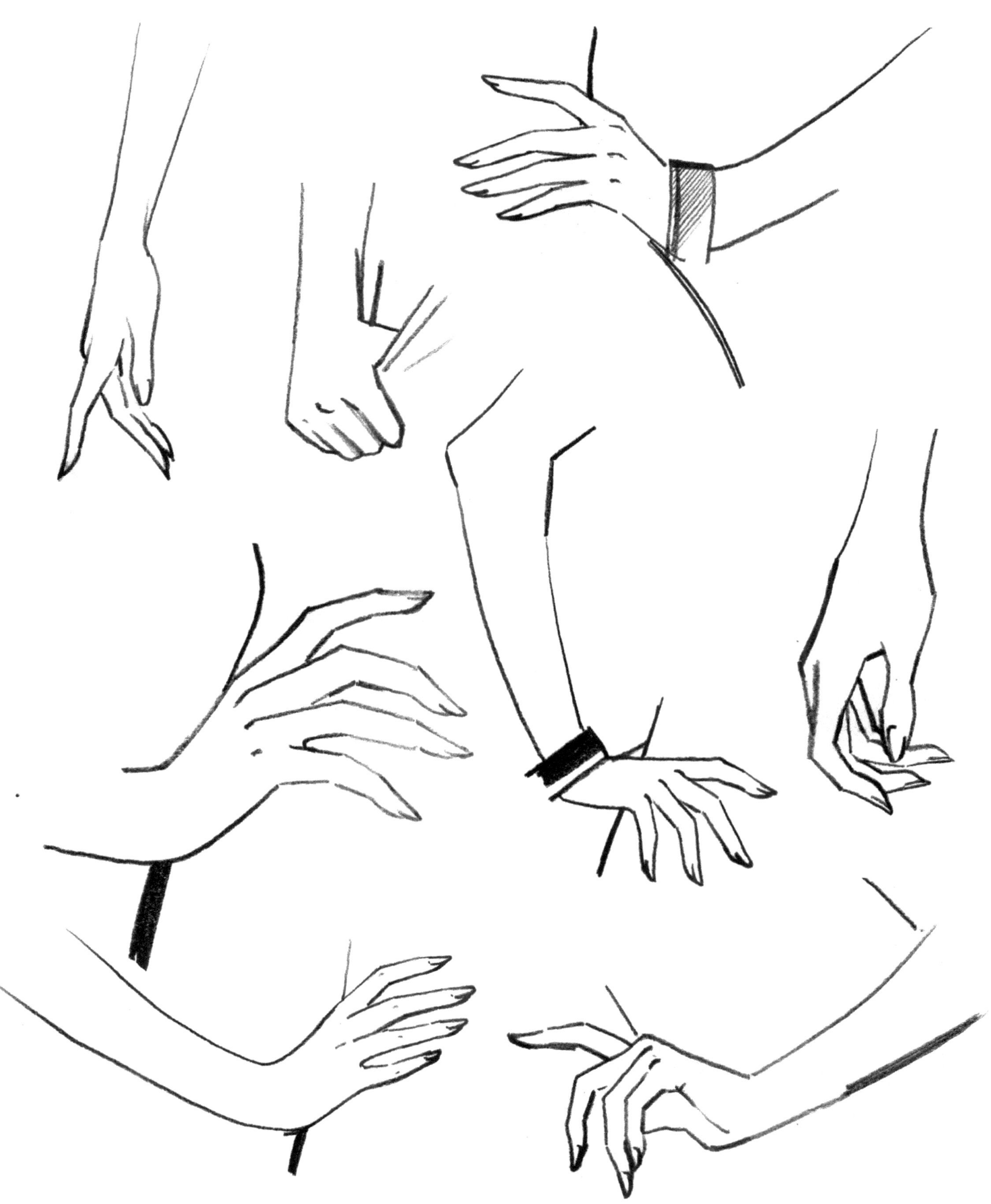

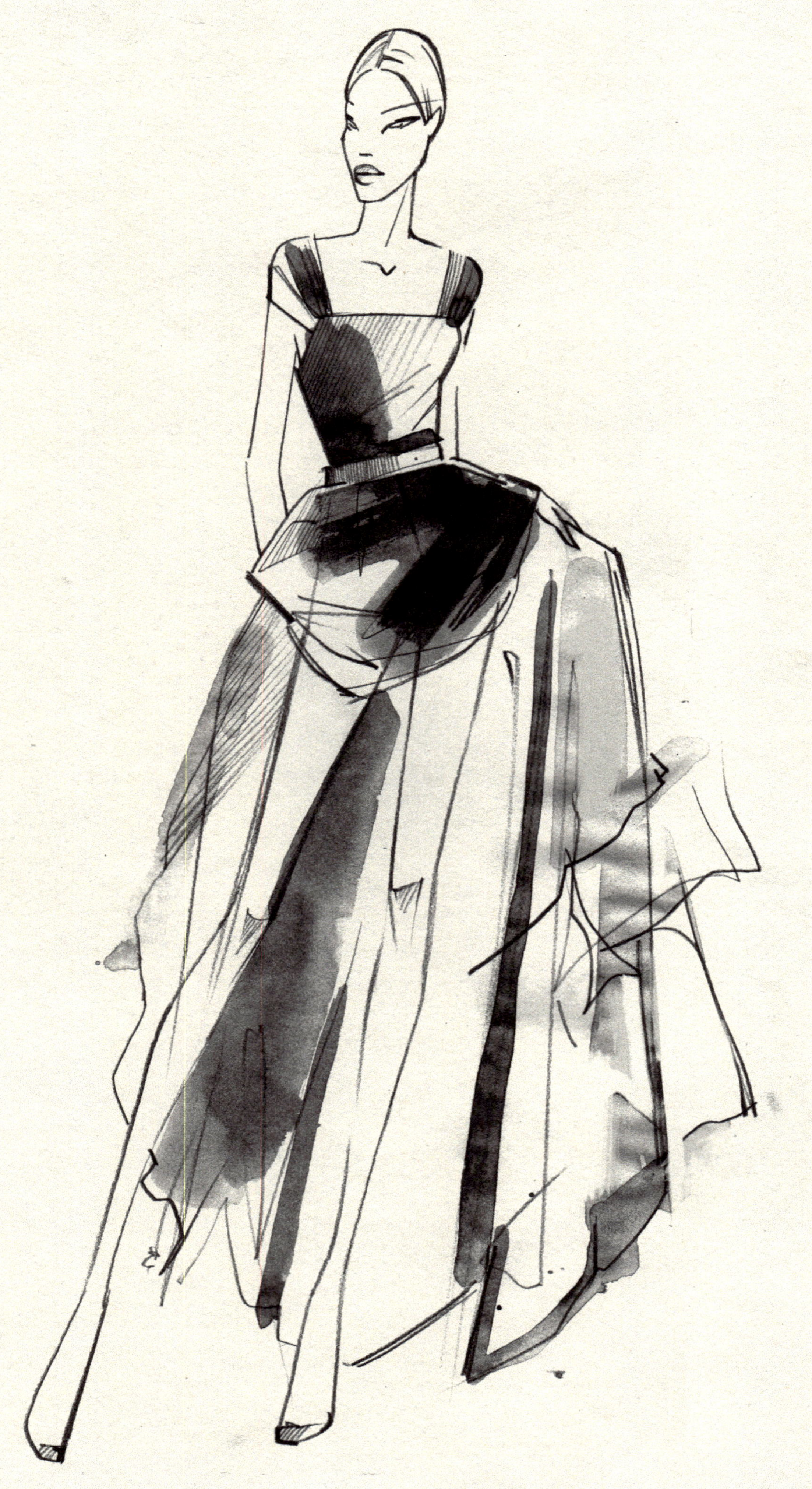

FEET

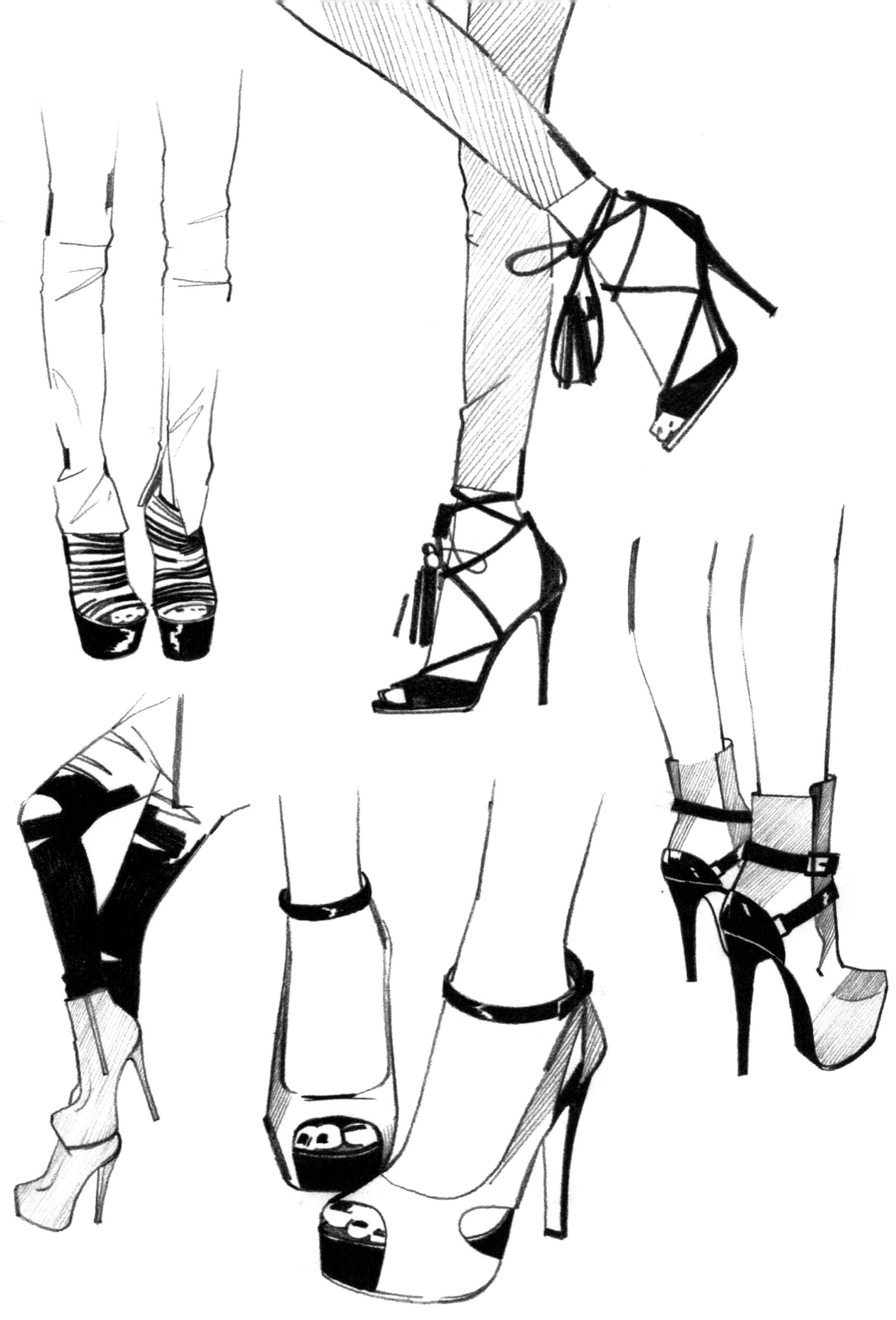

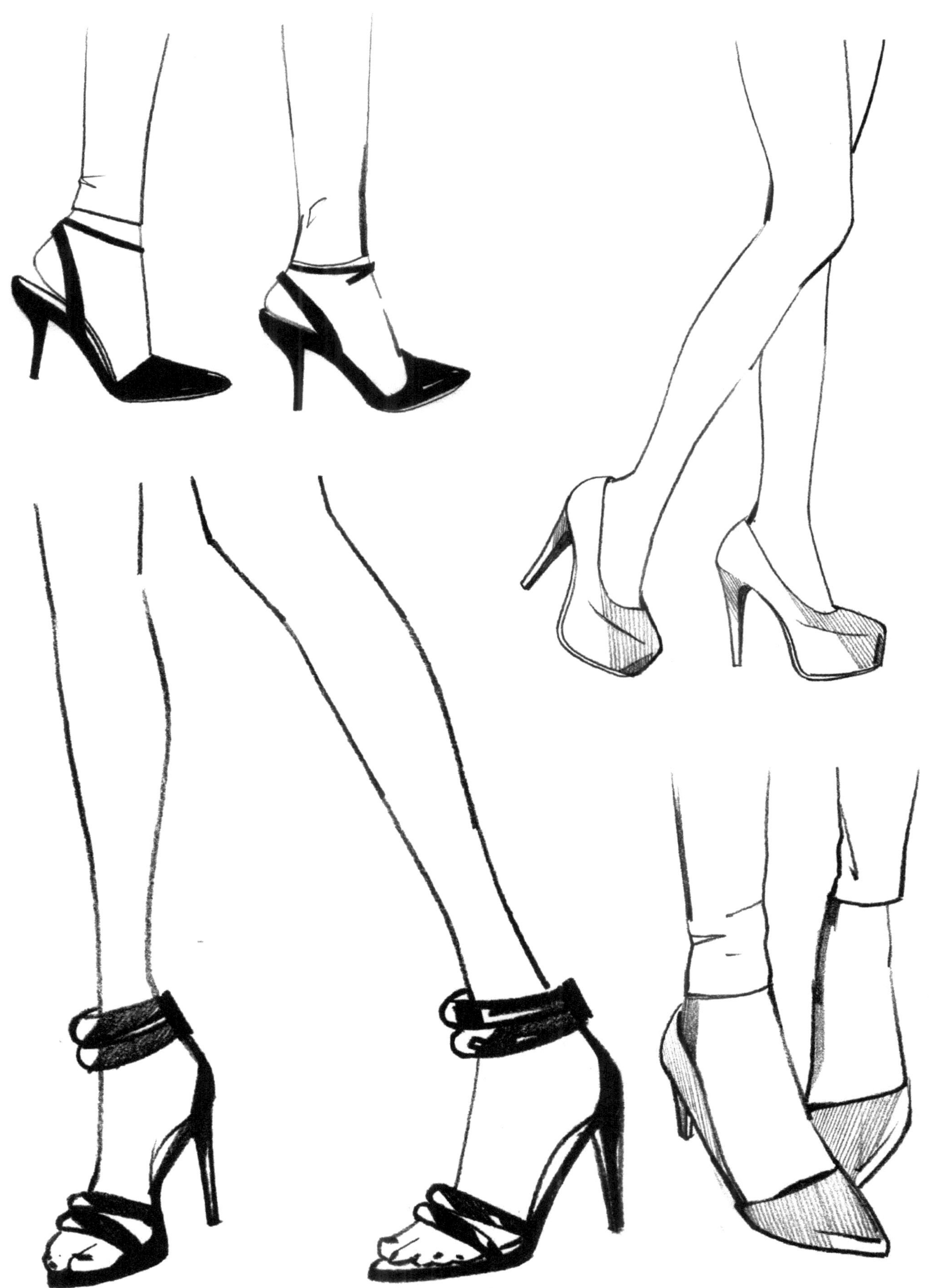

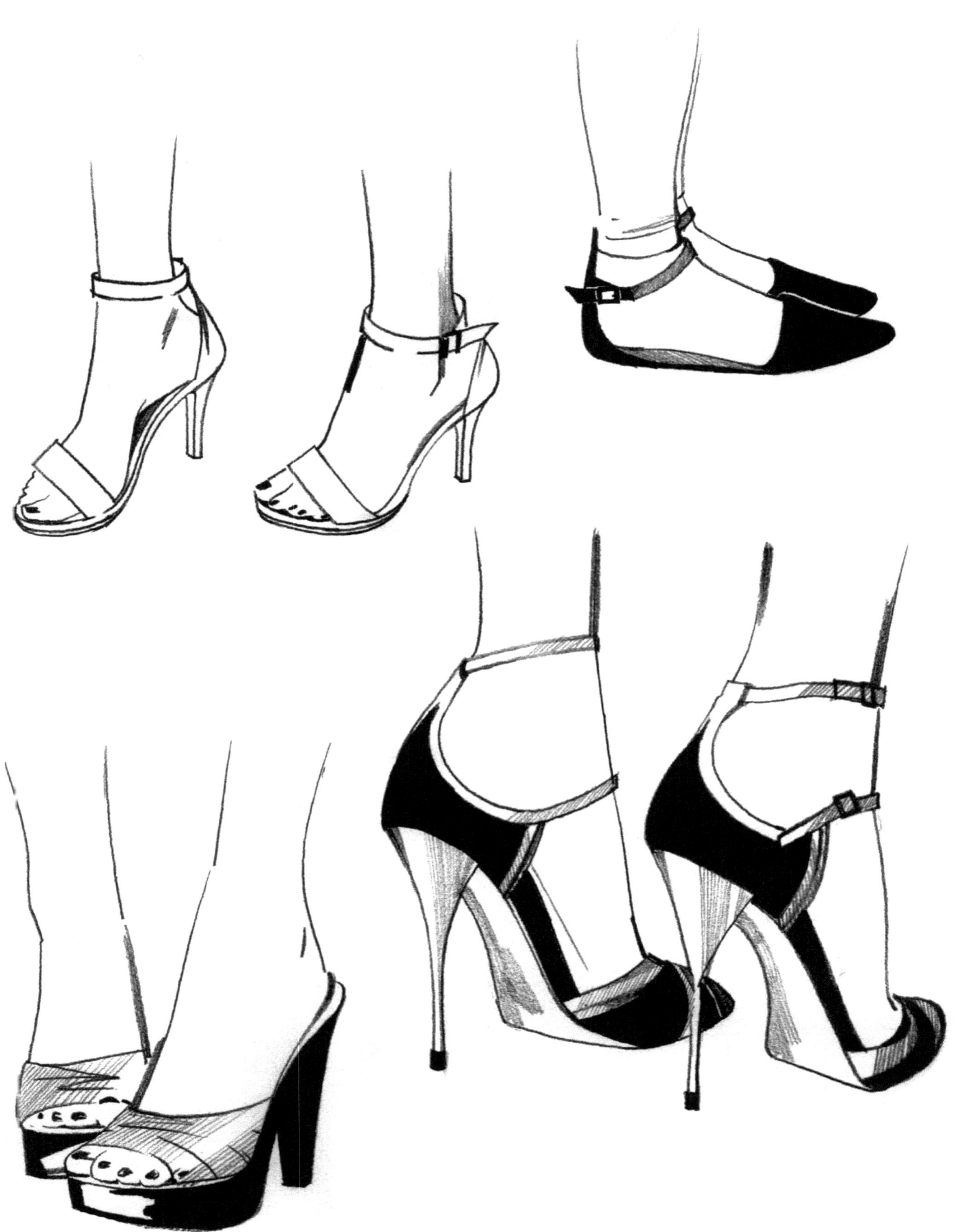

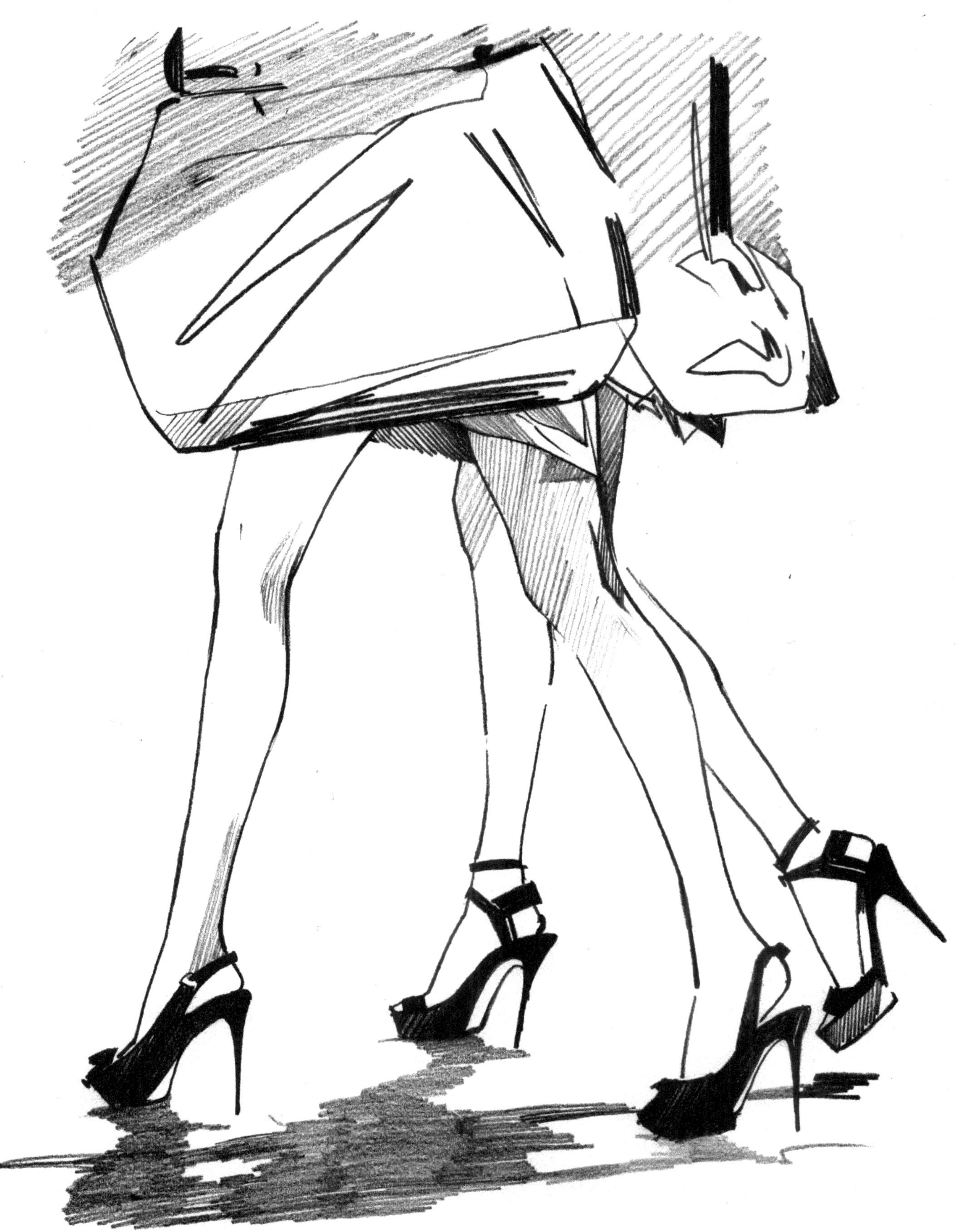

www.ingramcontent.com/pod-product-compliance
Ingram Content Group UK Ltd.
Pitfield, Milton Keynes, MK11 3LW, UK
UKHW060024300726
14090UKWH00019B/1074